SELL MORE

THE FORBIDDEN SECRETS
OF MASS PERSUASION

DAVE VANHOOSE

I dedicate this book to all the leaders willing
to step into their greatness, who have put in the time
and are willing to do the work to fulfill their call to
a greater future.

"Influencing others isn't luck or magic—it's science."
Robert Cialdini

"Make service rather than money your goal, and you will see the entire plan of your life change. You will never be left out."
Guruji Sri Sri Poonamji

CONTENTS

Welcome!

This book is only the beginning of your love affair with platform sales. There's a whole lot more fun and information for you over at DaveVanHoose360.com

Ongoing support and community are critical for success in any area of your life. One of the things that I learned is you become who you surround yourself with the most. One of the biggest factors in my on-going financial success, awareness, learning and growth has been sur-rounding myself with other smart, driven, successful and conscious people. I had a mastermind of people wiser than me, and it has helped me dramatically. I want this for you, too.

I've put together some resources, education, programs, tools and ongoing support for you. Join me and find out how you can surround yourself with other positive-thought leaders.

If you model what successful people do, you will become success-full. I believe in contributing & making a difference in the lives of the people I meet. When we work together, we will provide you with the absolute best speaker coaching & training to allow you to shine exactly as you are. Visit www.DaveVanHoose360.com to fast track your business success and join in on the fun and go deeper with the book.

A note to readers ...

This is going to be an unusual book, unlike any you've ever read before. Much of the content is taken directly from my platform speaking. I'll be communicating to you on three different levels.

First, on a base level, you'll read what you would hear if you came to one of my presentations; second, on a subconscious level, you'll learn about the hidden drivers that will have your audience running to the back table to buy; and lastly, at a superconscious level, we'll delve into the largely unknown techniques that have your audience interpreting the information you share with them at the subconscious level as rational and logical.

Say what? Simply put, superconscious experiences consist in becoming aware of the activity which is going on in the higher levels of the human consciousness. In other words, I fully explain to my audiences why they run to the back of the room to buy, they understand it completely, and they do it anyway. I make unconscious motivations available to the consciousness in a disguised form. We'll delve more deeply into why that's so cool in the later chapters.

How you can get the most out of this book: I recommend reading this book at least twice: the first time to learn the base-level techniques and mechanics of presenting and selling from the stage, and the second time to look for and understand the hidden techniques and covert commands I use in all my presentations. No matter what, you will understand the principles I teach and benefit at any level simply by reading this book.

***

Whatever you do, **make sure you read the first section of the book before you go to the Advanced Patterns.**

The techniques I teach in this book are controversial, and I invite you to open your mind up to possibility. As a neuro-linguistic programming practitioner, I know this to be true: your mind has set beliefs and belief patterns. Understand this—if I go outside the box of your belief, not only will you not believe me, you won't even consider believing me.

I encourage you to notice your reaction as you read this book— disbelief, disgust, anger, resistance—and understand that this is your belief system trying to keep itself intact and maintain the status quo. Not that long ago we thought the world was flat. If somebody had told you it was round, you wouldn't have believed it. I encourage you to open your mind to new ways of thinking, being and acting. Consider some new concepts and give these techniques the deliberation they deserve.

Take the strategies you like and disregard the rest.

INTRODUCTION

I get a text message on my phone. I pick it up and see a picture of a gold coin.

I'm confused. *Why is someone sending me a picture of a gold coin?*

And then it hits me. One night, about five years ago, I'm at an event. I see a woman, and for some reason I see right through her. I see pain and suffering deep behind her eyes. I realize I'm going to have to say something, but it's a challenge. When you have to confront somebody—really confront them with a truth they are unwilling to acknowledge for themselves—it takes guts.

I need to talk to you.

I sit her down and tell her I can see she's living with a lot of pain and suffering.

She nods. *You are right.*

We make a connection. She confesses that she is doing drugs and alcohol, that she's hurting herself, her family, her co-workers, and everyone around her. Our conversation lasts well into the morning. I leave her feeling empowered, with a message that helps her gain clarity, because she hasn't been able to see clearly for herself. She is transformed

within that conversation

If you had been a fly on the wall that night, you probably wouldn't have noticed anything unusual. But a trained ear would have noticed that I used the techniques you're about to learn in this book. Alcohol and drug addiction are very powerful patterns that are difficult to overcome, and statistics for sustainable change are grim. Within that conversation, I change her story. I change her patterns without knowing whether there will be long-lasting results.

I go on with my life and never see her again.

Now here I am in my office staring at a picture of a gold coin on my phone. The text message is from a colleague of mine in Costa Rica. It says, "Hey, I'm sitting here with a friend and I ask her who the most influential person she's ever met is, and her answer is *Dave Van Hoose!*"

I am stunned.

You guessed it; it's the woman I met five years earlier, and she's thanking me for taking the time to speak to her that night. She has been sober for five years, gone to school, completed her master's degree, and become a nurse. Her family has forgiven her. And because she quit drinking, her father, who was an alcoholic, also quit drinking.

In Alcoholics Anonymous you get a plastic chip for each anniversary of the day you stopped drinking. You also have the option of buying a more expensive chip to replace the plastic one. So here she is about to get another chip, and a 60-year-old woman says she got a message from God to bring her five-year chip to this event. She gives it to my friend. My friend cries thinking about everything she has been through and the lessons learned in her life. She takes a picture of the coin and sends it to me.

Why am I telling this story, and how does it relate to your "selling more"?

Conversations can do anything you want them to do. They can make you money; they can make you influential; they can change a life. Speaking from the stage is little more than having a conversation with your audience. The type of presentation I'll be teaching you in this book can be used for a variety of things: to help change bad behaviors;

to influence someone to buy your product or service; or to get the job of your dreams. It can be used to convince your soul mate that you are the one for them, to influence your kids to behave or do their homework. Speaking is a powerful tool.

Whether or not you want to admit it, you're selling in almost every conversation you have. So why not sell more? "Sell more" to get your kids to do their chores without complaining, to get upgraded to first class, to attract your ideal mate, sell more product, get more customers, more cash flow and more profits. How you sell more is all in the presentation. And if you get only one thing from this book, I want it to be this: in order to be successful, you've have got to *sell one to many*, and move away from selling one-to-one.

You are a speaker, whether you realize it or not. If you are talking to somebody on the phone, on a radio or TV show, or even to your kids or your employees, you are presenting a message. I do not care who you are; we all have the need to be persuasive and convincing when we speak. You never know whose life you are going to touch or when that opportunity is going to present itself. It is crucial to learn how to communicate if you are going to make a difference on this planet.

Speaking is a learned skill set. Using presentations while speaking is an art and a science. You are the artist and with the mathematical science behind presentations that I provide in this book, you'll have all the tools, information and skills you need to successfully sell more.

I break down my presentation into a step-by-step blueprint. I have developed incredibly effective systems, checklists, and procedures. I will share with you what to do on stage, show you the step-by-step system, and explain the techniques behind them. You are going to read about what happens behind the scenes when a speaker is on stage, the secrets, and all the techniques I've developed in the more than 3,000 presentations I've delivered. I have been called the "best closer" and the best salesman, but I know this for sure: if I can learn to do it, you can, too.

I promise you this: once you're done reading this book, you'll never listen to a speaker the same way again.

This system can be used for massive good, or it can be used for the ultimate evil. So I have to know that I can share this with you. Do you have a product or service or the intention of truly making a positive impact in the world? If your answer is no, please stop reading and put this book down.

Otherwise, put your hand on your heart and repeat after me:

I promise to use this information for good, to empower people, to get them out of fear, doubt, and confusion, and help them take the first important step of their life.

With that said, let's have some fun. Are you ready to dive into this?

chapter 1
WHAT IS SELLING?

"A good objective of leadership is to help those who are doing poorly to do well and to help those who are doing well to do even better."

—Jim Rohn, entrepreneur, author & motivational speaker

I couldn't even begin to teach the strategies of my blueprint without first addressing your views on selling. Take a minute to think about this. What is your primary emotion when the word 'selling' comes up? Most people have an overriding fear of it, or a driving desire to be liked and to 'look good'. They are afraid that selling is 'bad' or 'wrong' and that people will no longer like them if they don't agree with what they're trying to sell. So be honest with yourself. Do you think that selling is bad? Are you afraid of it? Are you worried what other people are going to think? What if you fail, what if you do it wrong, what if you are terrible at it? I'm going to let you in on a little secret: *you're not alone.* And congratulations, you're human. This is perfectly normal. And I can help you completely transform your relationship to selling.

I am going to ask you to open your mind to a new context around selling. Consider instead that selling is a service in which you provide value to another human being. Without somebody selling you something, you would not be holding this book. You wouldn't be sitting on your chair or living in your house, and everything around you would be empty. For those of you who don't want to be a hard salesman or don't feel comfortable closing, this is the perfect book for you.

I'm going to let you in on a little secret. I hated speaking and selling when I first started. Let me share a story with you.

One day I'm holding a *Foreclosures Daily* seminar in Tampa, Florida, for the National Association of Realtors. There are about 100 realtors in the audience, and I'm telling them the story of my first deal, where I made $42,000. I am listing every action step, showing them exactly how they can do this for themselves and how I can solve their problems. I am telling them how Foreclosures Daily will save them time, energy, and effort. At the end, I tell them to get up and go to the back of the room and take action now. And many of them don't. They are resistant. And I don't understand why they aren't all taking action when my product can clearly benefit them.

It hits me like a ton of bricks when I realize that they need more help that just learning the mechanics of how to buy and sell foreclosure properties. There is a deeper problem that is not being addressed and a more powerful and insidious driver. And it's this: *fear is running their lives and dictating their behavior.* The people coming to my seminars are not living the lives they want. They have credit card debt, financial and relationship difficulties, they are stressed out, overworked, and in bad health. They are in what I call a J-O-B, *journey of the broke.* I realize that the biggest problem they have is being afraid to step into their greatness. They're playing small! And they need my help to take action. So right then and there, I understand my audience in a way I never have before. From that point on, my relationship with selling completely shifts. I realize, ***I'm not selling, I'm helping.***

At that time, I was also teaching my staff about foreclosures, and I found out that the most important real estate was the six inches between their ears. I would tell them that the first deal was always the hardest; there was so much pain in it. I started doing a lot of timeline therapy work, taking people back to when they were kids and learning about their money beliefs. I would help people overcome their fears and phobias, their self-defeating beliefs about money and about communication. And of course that day I realized that the people at my events are in exactly the same situation. Of course I could teach my audience mechanics of foreclosures, the "how to", the action steps, everything they needed to be successful. But what really stopped them was their fear. Why not do what I did in therapy and bring it into my speaking? This is an entirely different level on which to communicate with somebody, and empower them beyond belief.

Today my context around selling is that it's a service I provide to empower and enable my audience to take action in their lives. From my 90-minute presentation, they are going to retain maybe one-half of one percent of what I am saying. Are they going to change their lives after one 90-minute teaching talk? No. Are you going to change their lives after you speak on stage? No. But if they act, and buy your coaching course, or come into your therapy course, or into your system, is that going to change their lives? YES.

This is why it's essential for you to reframe your context around selling before you read another page of this book. Help your audience discover value for themselves. Don't push them to do something they don't want to do; you get them to *take action toward something they already want*.

If someone has a phobia about swimming, that fear will stop them from ever going into the water. Your prospects also have a fear, the fear of taking action, of making their lives better. They wouldn't be in your audience if they didn't want to take action! And whatever is stopping them from 'going in the water' is what is stopping them in all areas of their lives.

I have been called the "best closer" and the best salesman, but at the end of the day, selling is a simple transfer of energy. That's all it is. In fact, selling should be an even exchange, so when we sell, we do not take advantage of others. We under-promise and over-deliver.

We've all heard the saying A-B-C, Always Be Closing. I want you to turn that phrase on its ear. Make a note of this: **A-B-H, Always Be Helping**. When you come from the intention to help, when you believe that you are there to serve and that your greatest service is by helping get them to take action, then there is no fear, and you can communicate and be empowered.

What I want to teach you is not closing, but starting. Starting people on a path, and starting them into what they want. They are coming to your classes. If they are in a bad relationship, going through a divorce, or having financial problems, they are not going to get help from the television or from colleges and universities. Help has got to come from you. You are the one starting them on the right path.

ABH will empower you with some amazing tools, because the ideas and the fear that are running through your audience have got them trapped. The majority are living in poverty, in fear, in doubt, so it's up to you to help them believe and empower themselves to take an action and a step forward to work with you.

What is the service you provide your audience? How can you empower and help them?

Like what you've read so far? Like us on Facebook!
www.facebook.com/DaveVanHoose

$$\text{\textcircled{\$}\textcircled{\$}\textcircled{\$}}$$

chapter 2
MY STORY

*"You gain strength, courage and confidence by every experience
in which you really stop to look fear in the face. You must do the thing
you think you cannot do."*

—Eleanor Roosevelt

Early Years

I grew up in Ann Arbor, Michigan, and I was the middle child. I had a rough upbringing. My parents got divorced when I was in the fourth grade and it was extremely difficult. They sent me to a Christian school, and I got held back in the third grade because I had dyslexia. This shattered my self-confidence as a young person, so I barely made it through high school. I acted out, and they put me in a resource room to try to contain me. I struggled. Growing up, I believed that I was worthless. When I turned 18, I graduated from high school with a 1.2 grade point average.

One day, I was sitting in the school counselor's office, and he looked at me and said, "So, Mr. VanHoose, what do you plan to do with the rest of your life?"

Now, my grandfather worked for 42 years with Henry Ford on the assembly line. My dad worked for 38 years for Ford Motor Company. I had a job at the factory loading semi trucks for UPS. I had never thought about that question, and I wanted to do what all the other kids were doing in Ann Arbor, Michigan. I said, "I want to go to college like everybody else."

And I'll never forget. He looked at me and laughed and said, "Mr. VanHoose, how do you plan to go to college with a 1.2 grade point average? You'd better keep your job at the factory." I walked out of his room with my head down, devastated. I walked home that day and thought to myself, "What am I going to do when I grow up?"

I decided right then and there that I was going to prove him wrong. I went to junior college and then got accepted into college, where I got a degree in sports medicine. I moved to Tampa, Florida. I was doing my internship at Morton Plant Hospital as a sports therapist. It was a very rewarding job. I helped people learn how to walk and move their extremities again. I was training and coaching people with injuries and within a year, I caught my first big break: a professional football team hired me to become a trainer.

This was an amazing opportunity. I got to travel the world. I was on ESPN TV. I worked with amazing athletes, empowering them after pain and injury to get back on the field and win championships. My entire life and my identity were wrapped up in what I did. In 2003, we won the XVII Tampa Bay Storm Arena Bowl World Championship, and I thought, "This is it. I've made it. I know who I am, I'm surrounded by greatness every day, I am living my dream."

And then I broke my back.

The injury was serious and the pain was overwhelming. I saw an orthopedic surgeon, Dr. Small. In his office, the doctor put my MRI and X-ray pictures on the board and said, "Dave, I see your problem is right here." I was only 29 years old and until now I had been in perfect physical shape. Now I could barely even stand or walk. He said, "Dave, you've got a broken back. You've got a Pars fracture at L5-S1 with a herniated disc."

Translation: You'll never walk again without pain.

I sat there staring blankly at him.

I'll never forget the next thing out of his mouth: "Dave, there's nothing I can do for you."

"At 29 years old, there's nothing you can do for me? What about surgery?"

"I'm not sure if surgery will work. I'm not sure if you'll ever walk again or function fully again." He thought I was too young for surgery.

I told him I wanted it anyway. I *demanded* a better life. He scheduled the surgery for two weeks later. They cut me through the anterior part of my stomach. They moved my organs out of the way and screwed my back together and put a rod and a cage in my back.

The day I woke up from surgery, time stopped. I was paralyzed. My legs were numb and I was in so much pain that even breathing hurt. The patient next to me cried all night long because he was in so much pain after his neck fusion. They put me on morphine. They put me on Demerol. I'm lying in bed thinking to myself, *What am I going to do now? What kind of career am I going to have? How am I going to walk?*

I remember the pain was so excruciating that I was in absolute terror. I thought my life was over. And to some extent, it was. Certainly, my life as an elite-athlete trainer was over. My whole life was shattered because I didn't know who I was without my career.

It was as bad as it gets.

The doctor said, "You've got to start sitting up. You've got to start moving." As a therapist I knew this, but as a patient I thought no way. I tried to roll over. Nothing. I tell him I can't do it. He says, "You have to." I used to think I was invincible. I thought I could do everything. But in that moment I remember believing that I couldn't do this. The simple task of rolling over seemed insurmountable. But the doctor said I would have to.

I rolled on my side and sat up, and he said, "Now you've got to learn how to walk again."

I said, "There's no physical way it's ever, ever going to happen." And again, he said I would have to. I took that first step. It was a long, painful process, but eventually I did start to learn how to walk again.

They sent me home in a wheelchair and my parents took care of me. My wife had left me because she didn't want to take care of me. She didn't want to deal with the repercussions of back surgery, or the lifestyle change that my convalescence would cause. I used to think that girls liked me because of my physique and my physical appearance. And there I was, 30 years old and living at my parents' house! They had bought a hospital bed for me to recover in. One morning I woke up and looked out to see my parents' swimming pool. I said to myself, "Dave, if you can learn how to walk just one time around that pool to get the extremities moving, you can learn how to walk again."

I still remember that first walk around the pool. They gave me a full-body cast. I put it on as tight as I could, stretching the Velcro as far as it would go to give me more back support. The cast dug into my incision wound and added even more pain. I took a cane and started to hobble around the pool like a 90-year-old man. It took me about half an hour to get around the pool that first day. The second day, I walked twice around, and the third day I made it around that pool three full laps.

Although there was physical progress, I was still worried about my future. *What am I going to do? My life is over.*

I didn't know how I was going to make it through the days. They had me on so many drugs for my pain, including morphine, Oxycontin, muscle relaxers, antidepressants, and sleeping pills. I was depressed, strung out, lonely and hopeless. I was at rock bottom. My whole identity had been shattered... I was an athlete and it was gone. Just like in high school in front of my high school guidance counselor, I had a choice to make. I could let this take me out, or I could step into something better.

So there I was walking around my parents' pool, thinking, *what can I do with the rest of my life, because I can't stand or sit for more than 20 minutes. What kind of career can I have?* All of a sudden, I had an idea. It almost took me over. *Maybe I can do real estate.*

I put the full-body cast on and drove down to the courthouse in Clearwater, Florida. There was a foreclosure auction that day, and I saw them auction a house for $100. *Man, I could have bought a house today for $100.* Little did I know they were selling it back to the bank, but I remember at the time being so envious. I so self-conscious, embarrassed because I was 30 years old and wearing a full-body cast and using a walker. I was humiliated. But I had this idea and it wouldn't let go of me. I took the foreclosure list and decided to do something with it. I flipped my first real estate deal and made $42,000.

Then I asked, *how can I reinvent myself?*

Who got rich during the gold rush? It wasn't the miners; it was the local merchant who sold all the equipment to the miners. I asked myself, *do I want to follow the gold or sell the picks, axes, and shovels?* That's when I had the idea, *what if we took these foreclosure listings and put them on a website and called it ForeclosuresDaily.com.*

And a new business was born.

How I Launched My First Business

I launched my first business on my credit card and started to build an online membership community. Now, I was getting ready to launch this new company. It was going to help people save time, energy, and money. It was the most innovative thing and I was so excited, I just couldn't believe what a great thing I had built. I was so jazzed. Guess how many customers I got the first month? Zero.

So I did what most entrepreneurs do—I made the product better. I launched it again. Guess how many customers I got? *Zero.* I had to find out how to get a customer.

I got good at communicating one to one, and then I realized, *why am I doing one to one; why don't I do one to many?* That's how I began in the seminar business, and right from the beginning, we used leverage in our business.

We hosted our first seminar at a Denny's restaurant with 12 people in the room and made about $2,000. The seminars were the way to do business. I wasn't the speaker at the time; I was the one who filled the room up. We had another speaker that came in and taught about foreclosures. We were like an event company. For me, I was happy to discover that the same high I got from sports I also got in the business world. Everything I did in sports, I did in business. There were a lot of similarities.

We were doing more and more events, and I remember clearly our first million-dollar month. I was over the moon. I was sitting in my office with my partner. Remember, my degree was in sports medicine. I didn't even know what a P&L statement is. (It's a profit and loss statement.)

Get this; we did a million bucks that month. What I didn't know at the time is that what's important isn't how much money you make, it's how much you keep. Our controller came in and said, "What are you guys celebrating?" I'm like, "We just made a million bucks, man!"

Out of that million dollars, guess how much was profit?

Zero.

We looked at the P&L statement with these things called expenses that I didn't know about. We were looking at the hotel rooms, the marketing costs, and then I looked at line item 32. We had outside speakers who would come in and sell and take fifty percent of the profits. *Fifty.* So, out of a million dollars, half would go to outside-speaker commissions.

My partner and I were sitting there and we realized, "Man, if we didn't have these outside speakers, we would have made half a million dollars this month. We could have been rich in one month." We decided right then and there that we needed to get our own system, create our own course, and have our own speakers. And who do you think this person was going to be? My partner and the controller both looked at me and said, "you're the one."

I was stunned.

"Me? No, no, no. Hold on for a minute. I'm not the one. I'm not a speaker."

But it was too late. The decision has already been made.

Looking back at that moment, I realize now that there was something running through my head. I went into complete fear. In third grade I had been held back. I had a belief running through my head that said I'm not good enough. But that wasn't going to stop me. I said, "You know what? I take the challenge."

My First Speaking Gig

I knew that I needed to be trained because I had been watching the speakers from the back of the room, and there was a system to it. So I went to a three-day speaker course to train in public speaking. My partners said to me, "Well, Mr. Speaker, we booked your first gig."

"Okay.

"Where is it?"

"In North Carolina."

"When?"

"Tomorrow."

Tomorrow!? I had just gotten back. We didn't even have our product done yet and the course wasn't finished. We didn't have my presentation; it was so premature. So if you're reading this and feeling like you're not ready, let me tell you, you'll never be ready. And speaking is always premature, so just do it. You will learn so much more from trying and failing than you will from living in fear and taking no action at all. And then do it again. And again. And again. And I promise you, you will get better and it will get easier.

> "Too many people spend too much time trying to perfect something before they actually do it. Instead of waiting for perfection, run with what you've got, and fix it along the way..."
>
> **Paul Arden, speaker & author**

I knew that speakers had to wear a suit, but I didn't have a suit. As a professional football trainer, I wore whatever shirt the sponsors provided me. I found a jacket and a tie. I didn't even know how to tie a tie, for goodness' sake. I went to the airport and flew to North Carolina.

My marketing manager at the time picked me up and drove me over. I sat in his car in front of the hall where I was to speak. It was getting dark and I was scared. My mind was racing and I was just praying for some force of nature to save me from having to speak. "Please, God, let there be a fire." I looked. No fire. "Please let there be a tornado, a hurricane, a snowstorm…*something, anything.*"

Nothing.

As I was thinking this, the guy next to me looked at me and said, "Dude, are you going to be okay? You're white as a ghost." The door squeaked as I slowly got out of the car. It felt like there were lead weights attached to my feet. I walked up to the hall, heart racing. I opened the door and saw about 300 people inside.

Signs had been created that said "Foreclosures Daily King, Dave VanHoose." And I was feeling even more pressure to perform. Because I was the speaker, all these people started pointing as I walked in. *They were pointing.* I used to be shy, so I ducked into the bathroom to pull myself together. I was so nervous they almost had to drag me out of there back into the room.

I was getting ready at the back of the room when the announcer said, "In a moment, I'm going to introduce Dave VanHoose. He flew all the way from Tampa, Florida, and today he's going to teach you how to buy and sell foreclosure properties. Let's give a warm welcome."

I ran up on stage and *wham!* time stopped. I got in the zone. I started sharing my passion with people, how I turned my life around after my first deal. I was teaching people exactly what I did, and I said, "Everybody get up right now and go to that table," *and they did.* Whew! We made $50,000 that day.

I was hooked.

Flying back, I was listening to Tony Robbins say, "I wasn't the best speaker in the world, and so I spoke four times a day, seven days a week." I told my partner, "Listen. I want to speak twice a day, seven days a week, to master this art." So I went out and did over 3,000 presentations. I started speaking twice a day, seven days a week, but I would lose my voice after the fifth day. I started speaking only five days a week. I asked everybody how to get my voice back, I tried everything, but no relief. That's when my company hit a bottleneck because Dave VanHoose could only do ten talks a week and that is it.

I needed to figure out how to duplicate myself. And of course the ego kicked in and said, "You can't duplicate me." I hired 25 speakers and started building my team. And that's when I created this powerful presentation blueprint that you're going to learn in the next chapter.

A necessary evolution in the growth of any business is building a team. The ego is going to try to say you can't duplicate yourself. I hear it all the time. Listen, I get it. Speaking is fun, and it makes us feel special and empowered. But sometimes we need to get ourselves out of the way. We built our team by doing what was best for the company, and within three years of starting the business, we made the *Inc. 500*. Imagine that. Within three years of my thinking my life was over, I was back on top, because I used the Sell More strategies that you're going to read about.

Flying High, Sinking Low

Now great things started to happen. Life was good. I admit I didn't have the leadership skills back then, so guess what I did? I bought a nice custom Hummer limo with a VIP section in the back. When that one was too big, I bought another limo with Lamborghini doors on it. Then I bought a 50-foot yacht, a condo on the water, and a bunch of stuff I didn't need. I was making all this money. I had an American Express black card. Life was sweet. I was on top of the world. I was living large. I put my whole identity into creating and being and living this celebrity persona.

Two big lessons I've learned. Lesson number one: looks don't matter. I used to think who you are is what you look like; then I broke my back and my looks didn't help me. Lesson number two: I thought who you are is what you have. And here's what happened: I lost it all.

I'll never forget this day. It was a Saturday in Tampa, about 85 degrees out. I got on my 50-foot yacht with some of my old football friends and ten or fifteen models. Some guys said, "Let's go out and race." We started up the engines and off we went.

This was a custom go-fast yacht called a Sunseeker Superhawk, one of the baddest, with three Yamaha motors. It actually said *Entourage* on the back, of course, because I let my ego run the show back then and bought it out of Miami from the president of Ecuador. I started up one engine, two engines, three engines. Everything was great.

I was out there racing this boat, shooting the rooster tail up. I was about two miles out in the ocean when all of a sudden, one engine completely died. I saw one of the engine gauges go completely down to nothing. Almost immediately, the second engine went down, and then the third. My buddy said, "Dude, hit the hatch." I hit the button that raises the engine cover so I could look. They were making this *ding-ding-ding* sound, and I saw salt water on these big diesel engines.

We're Going Down!

My buddy said, "Dude, we're sinking." "What? This is a 50-foot boat. This is bigger than my house." "We're sinking. Where's your flare gun?" I remember shooting the flare gun off, and the water was rushing into the boat. The whole boat tipped up, and we started to sink. Within five minutes, I was on the top of the boat with my cell phone and my wallet in hand. Somebody said, "Abandon ship!" I threw my phone in the water and jumped in.

The helicopter and Navy patrol picked us up out of the water. I couldn't believe it. Inside of 30 minutes, I had lost my beautiful boat and most of my pride. I watched the yacht go under as everybody got on the Navy patrol boat. I was devastated.

The sinking boat became a metaphor for my life. It was the beginning of the end.

Going From Hero to Zero and Back Again

I owned a limo company called South Tampa Limos. One day I called my partner, and he said, "Oh, yeah. By the way, I forgot to tell you. I haven't made the car payments and they just repossessed the limos."

I was sitting in my office and my partner said, "We're a couple of million dollars in debt. We've got payroll tomorrow, and we're going to bounce payroll." I'm telling you, when you bounce payroll to 100-plus people, it is a disaster.

Payroll bounced. The news crew came over; they did a bad story about us; and within three months of sinking that boat, I went from hero to zero. My house-buying business was going down in 2008. My limos, my house, my car, and every credit card were all repossessed. I had nothing. That's one of the main things I've learned. I was celebrating and valuing the wrong things, and I lost it all within three months.

I see a lot of people, myself included, who make lots of money but don't know how to handle it. I didn't have the self-discipline, the maturity, or the emotional sobriety. When we had to lay off 100 employees, I cried. It was the most horrifying thing I've ever had to do.

So there I was. Broke. Hated. In debt. What was I going to do next? My house was in foreclosure. I was Mr. Foreclosures Daily and *my house was on my own list and all my customers were going to see it.* Here I was again, trying to figure out, *what am I going to do? I can't go get a job.*

Then two words popped into my head. *Sell More.* And I remembered who I am. I am Dave VanHoose. I am a speaker. I still have enthusiasm. We took our company to the Inc. 500. I've done all these presentations. And speakers don't know how to present, salespeople don't know how to convert, Thought Leaders don't know how to communicate their message, and entrepreneurs don't know how to build their businesses.

So I joined forces with my current business partner, Dustin Matthews. We created our new company. We were 50/50 owners, and we used his credit card to start the business because, as you know, I had nothing left. And that's what we did. Through the knowledge and the mindset that I created and the marketing and expertise that Dustin brings, we came back. Within a very short time, we got to a million dollars again; we were working with all the top speakers, speaking on the Get Motivated circuit; and we were having lots of fun following Zig Ziglar.

chapter 3
WHAT IS SELLING MORE?

"Less is more only when more is too much."

—Frank Lloyd Wright

Selling more leads to more of everything: serving, more customers to help, more changes in lives, more cash flow in your business to build a sustainable organization; selling builds insurance plans for your employees, a better lifestyle for your employees, and more wealth and freedom for you and your kids. Take a look at what I call my Sell More Formula.

Trust + Value + Messaging = Sale

This formula is as straightforward as it gets. First and foremost, you've got to get prospects to trust you. After establishing trust, give them value. Then add messaging -- how what you're communicating is going to bring you to the sale.

Establish Trust

In my seminars, I always demonstrate trust by doing the $100 bill exercise. I get someone to come up and give me a $100 bill. I explain to them that they're not going to get anything in exchange. I take their $100 and ask them to sit back down. Now remember, they have no reason to expect that they are going to get anything in return for the $100 they just gave me. That audience member has given me money for no reason.

This exercise accomplishes two things: one, it establishes trust and two, it shows my audience how they can create value out of thin air. Some of my audience members are just starting their business ventures and don't yet have any products created. If you are reading this and thinking the same thing, here is an example pulled straight from a transcript of one of my live events:

> **Dave:** *How many in this room actually trust me? Quick, put your hands up. Now how many people in this room who trust me have a $100 bill in their pocket? Raise your hands. Okay, if you have a $100 bill in your pocket, take it out and stand up if you trust me. Wave it up nice and high. We talked about trust plus value plus the message equals the sale.*
>
> *So who trusts me and has got a $100 bill? Who in this room would give me their $100 bill right now? Come on up here. Now I have nothing to offer you. Is that okay, still?*
>
> *Do you trust me?*
>
> **Audience Member:** *I trust you.*
>
> **Dave:** *Okay, great. You can go ahead and sit down. Trust, as you can see, is very important for sales, right? So step number one, I had trust. Just by trust alone, we can get a sale. Now we need value. You might say, well, I don't have a product. Who in this room right now does not have a product or service or is not sure what their product or service is? Put them up; let me see your hands nice and high.*
>
> *For you guys, let me share how easy this will be. You gave me $100, thank you. Now here's what I want to do. I want to build*

value for her for that exchange. Who in this room would offer up something as value for her for taking action, making a commitment?

X: [An audience member says what they have of value to give her.]

Dave: *Awesome, and how much do you charge for that?*

X: $500

Dave: *Does anybody else have anything else for value that we can offer?*

[Various audience members offer products and services, such as a coaching session and a radio appearance, worth $680, $750, $4100, $1197, $6600, $12,000, $25,000, and more, until the total value created exceeds $50,000.]

Dave: *Wooo! Let's give everybody a hand for playing. Come on up here. So now, I want to give you your $100 back for playing. Let's give her a hand. {applause} Just promise me, the people who said they're going to commit, just get with her at lunch, so we can make sure to get it, and thank you very much for playing.*

Using the Sell More techniques, we were able to build more than $50,000 in value for this person who trusted me enough to give me a $100 bill. True learning occurs by demonstration.

Create Value

So even if you don't yet have a product, you likely know people who have products or services, and you can create value through the people you already know! Start joint ventures, become an affiliate. Sell someone else's product or service to people who trust you. Most of us get caught into only selling our own product or service. I always focus on the client, and getting them results. Create a results-driven business, and you will have an abundance of customers.

Foreclosures Daily was just a company that put together a list of foreclosures. Most of the people who got the list did nothing with it. I thought, *What do these people need in order to act?* Since they got the list, they probably have marketing tools to get out to the people in foreclosure. I found the company that does the best marketing via automated mailers. I found a company that would take my foreclosure list and mail the materials to the people listed.

I put those services into my program, and then I went further. Most realtors and most investors use the mail to contact people involved in foreclosures, and these realtors and investors are not answering their phones. So I found a company that would answer phone calls, talk to the people in foreclosure, type out all the information, and send an e-mail to the realtors and investors that said "Hey, I have somebody in foreclosure, they want to talk to you." Does that sound cool?

I added that to my system. Then I realized these guys do not have the necessary forms when they put the property under contract. So I found an attorney and I said, "Listen, you've got paperwork, and I know you're looking to get more customers. Would you put your paperwork into my course for free, thinking that people will get your paperwork and might want to hire you for more services?" He said yes, so I added the forms and contracts. Finally, I'm thinking they need to come to a training session, a boot camp where I teach them step by step how to do it. I did not want to teach the boot camp, so I asked one of my customers who was good at buying and selling foreclosures to teach the boot camp. Hint, hint.

This is how we investigate what we are offering up and create what my business partner Dustin Mathews is the master of, *the irresistible offer.* So now we've got trust, and you now know how to create value. Do you have a product or service, or a boot camp, or coaching that could be added to somebody else's system so you could get buyers to know who you are?

If you are not the greatest speaker but you have the greatest package and the greatest offer, will it convert more sales? *Absolutely.* Especially today, when most people have products that do not even work, there is an even greater need for value-driven products. You will be able to differentiate yourself. In fact, put this at the forefront of your mind—overpromise and overdeliver. I want your customers to say it's the best experience they've had among all the presentations they've seen. I want you to be able to deliver a powerful presentation and to overdeliver on the promises you made in the presentation.

Messaging

How do we create the right message?

Ninety percent of the people in this industry will go out of business in five years or less. I have seen businesses making $100 to $200 million go out of business a year later. So I investigated why this was happening. After four years of research, I can tell you the number one reason why most businesses in this industry fail within five years or less is simple: they can't service their customers or manage their business. It's a dysfunctional sales process. You're not going to get a customer if you don't know how to deliver your message. Nobody is going to buy your product. *If you can't get a customer, you're going out of business.*

> "People do not understand. They may have the best product in the world—they could have the cure for cancer—but if they can't convert a presentation or product into a sale, they are in deep trouble."
> **Rich Schefren,**
> **CEO, Strategic Profits**

I don't want you to be a statistic. That's why I'm going to be very aggressive. Most other speakers in this industry don't know what they're doing. They don't know how to get on stage and communicate their message. I see so many people who are not being converted on their webinars. I see many people who don't know how to anchor down their product. They lack automation in their system. That's why I developed my mathematical blueprint. I'm going to walk you through it, step by step by step, how to write your webinar or stage presentations, what I call the core story of your business. You've got to have a message, a core story, for your product or service. This core story can be used on the stage, on a webinar, on a product launch, on the sales floor, or talking one to one, but you've got to have an effective core story presentation.

Let me share a quick story about one of our clients who is a Thought Leader so you can learn from his mistake. He had talked to a promoter in Las Vegas and had a product that was ideal for the audience. This is a dream scenario: the perfect product for the perfect crowd. It should have been a homerun. He came to one of my training sessions, and I told him he needed to come in for my Power Day so I could teach him exactly how to package his product in the most effective way. He didn't think he needed this system. He was in the entertainment business and thought he knew what he was doing. I said, "All right."

He was speaking and got to the end of his presentation and told everyone to get up and go to that back table. Nobody did. The worst thing that can happen to a speaker who's a salesman is that nobody buys. He wasn't trained and didn't use the tools you're going to learn in this book. He called me that night because he knew I could help him. I immediately got him into our training program. We scripted out his presentation, and he rehearsed it word for word. He's made $3 to $5 million per year from that presentation. He tells me he's really taken his business to the next level. He speaks all over the world. Having now mastered these skills and techniques, he's about to take his business public.

SECTION 1
THE BLUEPRINT

chapter 4

THE SELL MORE PRESENTATION BLUEPRINT

"All wealth is based upon systems."

—Dan Kennedy, author and marketing coach

If you want to be the best, you've got to be scripted. If you're reading this and you still think that you don't know if you want to be scripted, consider this: Think of one of your favorite bands or singers. And then think of your favorite song by that singer. How many times do you think he or she has sung that song? Thousands. And when you hear her sing it, it sounds like the very first time. It's the same for a professional speaker. You have a script, and you make it come alive like it's the very first time, every time.

In my old Foreclosures Daily talk, I only had 90 minutes. When you do a 90-minute presentation, know that every second is like a year, that's how tight it's got to be. I was so scripted that every action was engineered precisely into my talk. I knew at exactly what moment to pick up my glass of water and drink it to achieve the power of pause, that's how scripted I was. That's why I was so lethal.

Science Behind the System

My job is to get you to be the number one speaker, salesperson, and thought leader on every stage. Now that you have this blueprint, you'll consistently be one of the top speakers at every speaking event, or the top salesman in your industry.

I'm not asking you to be me. Make this presentation your own. When you understand the science, you can step in and be the artist. You still get to generate the intention. Being the artist, you have to speak from your heart. You want to be extremely authentic when you present. You want to make sure you have integrity. You want to make sure you have magnetism. I can teach you how to have magnetic power on stage, but you have to come with the intention to serve and be 100 percent transparent with people. That's your job as the artist, and you've got to speak the truth. The truth vibrates at a higher frequency and will impact more people than anything else that you can do.

As I mentioned at the start of this book, when I first started speaking, I was the worst speaker on the planet. I stuttered; I looked down all the time instead of looking at the audience; I really struggled at it. However, I focused on the same strategies that had helped me excel in sports: I practiced the mechanics. Everyone is capable of learning mechanics.

You have to master this skill if you want to be successful. It takes a lot of courage. When I see people present their message badly, all I can think is, "Oh my gosh, they've got to get here and get with me because

I can help them fix that." This is an easy, predictable, scalable, track-able system. The blueprint consists of five parts. I have broken down each of the five parts of the Blueprint into its own chapter:

Part I: Intro
Part II: Story
Part III: Offer
Part IV: Body
Part V: Close

Download your own copy of the
Sell More Presentation Blueprint by going to our website
www.DaveVanHoose360.com/blueprint

chapter 5

PART I: INTRO

When you advertise fire-extinguishers, open with the fire."
—**David Ogilvy, advertising executive**

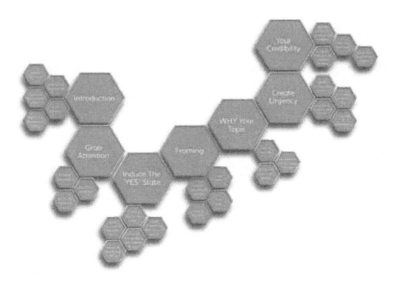

Introduction

Have a Leader Introduce You/Have Leader Transfer Power

I will share with you one strategy that will almost guarantee you will be the best speaker on every stage. If you happen to be speaking on the big circuit, they'll usually have an emcee introduce you. At best, the emcee is going to do a mediocre job.

Here's a better strategy.

Let's say you're speaking at a Tony Robbins seminar. You come up to him and say, "Hey, Tony, would you mind introducing me from the stage and tell that story about how I trained your son, and a lot of your coaches?" What do you think he's going to say? Of course he's going to say yes! And why is everybody in that room at a Tony Robbins seminar? Because of Tony! He is the trusted advisor. When Tony speaks, they listen.

When Tony comes up on stage, he'll say something like, "In a moment I'm going to introduce Dave VanHoose. Dave is somebody who's trained my son and a lot of my top coaches, and today he wants to share with you how to add speaking to your business. Let's give him a warm welcome." Here's the key. As soon as I come up on the stage I want to get a handshake or hug so the **transition of power** is made to me. Now I'm their trusted advisor, so when I speak they listen.

Use An Intro Video

When it's not possible to have a leader introduce you, I use an intro video to bring me up on stage. My friend Larry Benet at SANG (Speakers & Authors Networking Group) had me come and speak to his organization. For me, it's the perfect scene: Tony Robbins is there, Jack Canfield is there, Mark Victor Hansen is there, all the best speakers in the world are there. They had me come and speak about speaking to the speakers. There were millionaires and billionaires at this event, so the challenge was to establish trust in a room full of the highly in-

Want to see Dave's intro video?
Go to
DaveVanHoose360.com

fluential. I created an intro video. I played it and when I got up on stage, I got a standing ovation. I didn't have to grab their attention. I didn't have to build rapport. That video was 2 minutes and 30 seconds long. The sell happened before I showed up. I probably made an extra $800,000 from a $5,000 video. Was that a smart strategy? Could we all have an intro video? Absolutely.

Grab Attention

> *"Attention is vitality. It connects you with others.*
> *It makes you eager. Stay eager."*
> **-Susan Sontag, novelist & activist**

Control the Audience

Have you ever seen a speaker get up and the audience asks questions and ends up taking over? When the audience takes over, the speaker loses his power. As a speaker, you have always got to take control and keep the power. If you are speaking and something crazy or unexpected happens -- like the lights go out, the projector stops working -- stop, take a deep breath, make a joke about it, and move on.

By using the Sell More techniques in this book, you'll learn to control the audience's physiology. I do this by getting them to stand up and sit down, laugh and have a joke. You don't want to talk "at" the audience; you want to use nonresistant communication, which we'll talk about more in the Advanced Chapter of the book.

Here is a sample transcript I use from my Sell More Summit:

> *Now I've got a really cool, amazing strategy. How many of you want me to share a strategy with you right now that will put more money in your pocket? {show of hands}. How many of you are really serious?*
>
> *If you are, stand up for a moment. Watch me very closely and listen. Everyone stretch your hands out in front of your body. I want everybody to turn to the right and watch me closely. Take*

your right hand. I'm going to share with you a strategy to put more money in your pocket. Reach out and grab the wallet of the person beside you and put it in your pocket.

I know this to be true—the mind controls the body. Chiropractors and therapists know that if you control the body, you'll control the mind. They are connected. By having the audience stand up, they are taking your direction and giving you their agreement. Essentially, they are committing to you. ***Small commitments equal big commitments.*** So if you want to grab control, get your audience to stand up **at least once** during your presentation, before you ask them at the end to stand up and buy at the back table because you controlled their physiology. If they did it once, they will do it again.

Bring Audience Into Conversation & Excite the Imagination

Most people will get up on stage and want to talk "at" the audience, kind of like a football coach talks to kids. That is a bad strategy. A better strategy is to excite the imagination of the audience and bring them into your conversation. People buy into emotions. We've got to really get emotional with them, and help them see the emotion.

I'm going to teach you some language patterns, some trigger words. One of the best ways I know to do this is by using *Have you ever wondered?*

This is how it works:

> *Have you ever wondered what it would feel like to wake up every single day and know that your business is running on autopilot?*
>
> *Have you ever wondered what it would feel like to have qualified leads coming to your salespersons and a complete system?*
>
> *Have you ever wondered what it would feel like to travel the world or spend more time with your family as your business made seven and eight figures?*

You're grabbing the attention of the audience and bringing them into your conversation. You want to excite their imagination.

Induce a Yes State

7 Yeses = A Sale

All successful salespeople know that seven yeses equals the sale. The first Sell of any presentation is getting the audience to agree with you. This is what's known as the Yes State. Think of this. The audience can do one of two things. They can agree with you, or they can disagree with you. You want small agreements throughout the presentation. We want them to say yes, yes, yes, yes.

What is the number one reason most people go to seminars? To make more money! Ask them simple easy questions that are easy for them to say yes to so you can start building connections with them.

What does a speaker say to get everybody to say yes? Here's a sample script of how to induce a yes state with your audience:

By a show of hands, how many people want to make more money? Put them up and say yes! Awesome! By a show of hands, how many people today want me to share with you a proven step-by-step system that will virtually guarantee you financial freedom? Put 'Em up and say oh yeah! By a show of hands, how many today want to get the most out of our time together? I want that for you.

Three yeses, they're sold. Remember, small commitments will equal a big commitment.

Always Be FUN to Say Yes To

When your audience is entertained, they're lulled into trusting you. Resistance goes down, they can relax. Having fun creates trust and affinity. Fun = money.

Force a Response When One Is Missing

Understand there's going to be a lack of response when you start this. People aren't naturally inclined to agree with you. There's going to be resistance. Half the audience will raise their hands, the other half won't. So you've got to create a strategy to get them involved and get everybody to agree with you. We know that the words we use in our presentation are important. What's more important is your body language. When you start inducing the yes state, I want you to use your body, and I want you want to overemphasize. If you think you're overemphasizing too much, you're not doing it enough. When you start the yes state, remember that you're giving a command and you want a response from them. That's called conditioning. Write this down: **As a speaker, you're conditioning the audience to respond to you.**

Sometimes that means asking the question more than once. I say:

> *"By a show of hands, who in this room wants to make more money? By the way, if your hand isn't up, you can get up right now and leave."*

If you use that technique, make sure you say it in a joking, laughing manner.

> *"How many of you want to make more money, how many of you want to make NO money, how many of you aren't going to say anything no matter what I say?"*

Small Commitments Equal BIG ONES

If you can't get them to agree with you or answer simple, easy engagement questions, they're not going to run to the back of the room.

When you start the yes state, and you're asking these questions, you want to get off the stage, and come down to the level of your audience, touch your forehead, and get up on your tippy toes. I see so many people who do it half-heartedly and without conviction, as if they're not entirely certain, and the audience is confused. It's a very important part of the presentation. You want to give a command and you want to get the response, and then—and this is a super ninja strategy—you acknowledge them.

Framing

- Future Pace
- Tell 'Em What You're Gonna Tell 'Em
- Make a Promise

Framing is telling people what they're about to experience. The bigger the frame you create, the better off you are.

Our minds are like computers. When you install software into a computer, the computer reads the software and follows the instructions. Software consists of clearly defined instructions that, upon execution, tell the hardware to perform the tasks for which it is designed. Software is stored in computer memory and cannot be touched. The same thing goes for the mind! Whatever suggestions we give the mind, it will do.

Many of my clients are doing many of the things I'm teaching in this book, but in the wrong order. Are you doing webinars right now and you're listeners are dropping off before the end of the call? Here's what you can do: you can set a bigger frame. The bigger the frame you set, the more likely you are to have an audience that will stay on until the end. So how do you do that? **When you are speaking, tell your audience what they're about to experience,** and when you do, they will experience it. Let me give you an example. I did a lot of therapy work as a hypnotist. I would put the conscious mind to rest to go into the subconscious to find the belief pattern I had to change. For therapy, maybe it was a fear, a phobia, or a relationship.

So I would frame the pattern in what is called a hypnotic induction, a trance, just by saying the following: "In a moment, I'm going to begin counting backwards from ten to one. The moment I say the number ten, your body will begin to relax." They'd go right into a trance. That's a frame. We can use the same strategy in our speaking. We can set the frame of what they're about to experience. Here's an example. Let's say you are speaking on relationships:

> *"I'm so excited to be here at Harvard University to teach you about relationships. What you're about to discover is how relationships impact your life. Today, right here, right now, I'm going to share with you how to improve your relationships. In a moment I'm going to talk to you about how your programming from the past is affecting your relationships today. I'm going to share with you how to find the perfect soul mate and how to have relationships and partnerships for life."*

Would that get you? The bigger you set the frame, the more engaged they're going to be.

Open Looping

Now pay attention, because what I'm about to say is really important: Open loops create credibility, entice curiosity and will stimulate the brain's need to know more. When you set open loops, the mind naturally wants to close those loops. Three-times bestselling author Robert Allen once told me the most important thing he ever learned about speaking, and I can't wait to share it with you. But first let me get back to open looping.

See what I did there?

The purpose of an open loop is to maintain interest. People are naturally curious. If you say something that sparks the listener's curiosity and then don't close off that curiosity, you can hold their attention for a really long time. The front page of every newspaper is an open loop to get you to read the articles inside.

Larry Benet asked me to speak at the Speakers, Authors, Networkers Group conference. I had just started speaking at the time, so I wasn't well known as a speaker-coach yet. I was known as the owner of one of the most successful real estate education companies and one of the top closers in that industry. It was a big deal for me. Larry said to me, "You can't sell." I said, "Don't worry. I won't sell." What's funny is I got up there and I wanted to play a game. I wanted to see if these guys would get it because they're speakers. So I framed them and open-looped them to death.

> "My name's Dave VanHoose and in a moment I'm going to teach you how to present your message at a completely other level from the platform. I'm going to share with how you anchor your product down. Today I'm going to share with you how to anchor down a back table Today I am going to talk to you about subconscious communication. I'm going to share with you a technique I call NEEP. I'm going to teach you x. I'm going to show you y. We're going to go over this. In a moment I'm going to do this. I'm going to show you this."

Hook, hook, hook, hook, hook, hook, hook.

At the end of my presentation, they had to fill in those loops. If you're teaching from the stage and you fill in all the loops, there's no anticipation left to make an action. If I tell you what Robert Allen said at the end, there's no reason to listen to continue listening or reading. So, in your presentation, don't be afraid, especially on a webinar, to really set the frame in open loops.

Future Pacing

If you can, always take people down a path. Sell your audience on the next slide, on what's coming next. Speak in the present tense. Take them from the now into the future with you. In my old Foreclosures Daily presentation, I was constantly leading the audience. They would be following but they couldn't keep up with the pace. It was like they could never catch me. The result is that they'd be hanging on to every word. You're taking them on a journey. You can say things like this: "How many of you are liking this? Well, I've saved the best for last."

You lead the audience by making your presentation about the future:

- *In a moment*
- *What you're about to see*
- *In a second*
- *Today we're going to talk about*
- *Here's what we're going to do*

That will captivate the audience. Are you following me on that? You'll see in the next section how important it is to always sell the next slide.

WHY Your Topic

One of the biggest challenges that presenters and salespeople have is focusing on the audience rather than making the presentations about themselves. You always need to make it about them. The best way to do that is by answering the questions **"Why should I buy this? What's in it for me?"**

Get Audience Excited About Topic/Industry

Be very transparent. Too many presenters beat around the bush. Tell them exactly what's in it for them, and why they should buy your product or service. If it's about real estate, sell the benefits, let them see your vision. The more up-front and transparent you are, the better you will do.

Benefits of Your Topic/Industry

Why automate, why build an online funnel? So you can build your business on autopilot. Why? So you're not local, you're global. Why? So you can get more customers. Why? So you can have financial freedom.

Create Urgency
Sell Why the Opportunity Is Now

Why now? Because if, at the end of your presentation, they don't run to the back to buy, are they ever going to buy? Probably not. So we've got to get into action when? Now.

You've got to get your audience to a yes or a no answer, never a maybe. A maybe is just a smokescreen, a way to string you along.

What you've got to do here is show them the pain of not signing up. What is this costing them? Until you put that into your presentations, people are not going to take action. People want to play ordinary and small, but your job is to get them to open up and play big.

Your Credibility

> *"People buy into the leader before they buy into the vision."*
> —**John C. Maxwell**

When you're presenting your message, you have got to become the authority or the expert. In your presentation you have got to have a credibility slide that will position you as the authority and the expert.

You'll have instant control and instant power by including your credentials in you PowerPoint or Keynote presentation.

- Your Past Successes/accomplishments/Awards
- TV, Media, Past Deals, and Internet Presence
- What Sets You Apart
- How You're an Authority Figure

Last year I got a call from a friend in London saying that one of his clients was putting on a conference called *The World Speaking Summit*. All the top speaking-trainers in the world would be there. And my friend said to him, "You've got to have Dave VanHoose, he's the best in the world, he's my coach, and I love him."

So this client calls me up and says, "Hey, I'm doing a big event, I'd love to have you come and speak." Okay, no problem. I fly to London, and when I get there, there are 17 other selling speakers there. I didn't know this, because I didn't ask the question. And had I known I would not have shown up, because I'm not going to be a part of any pitch fest. No value, it's not me, I'm not in that place.

I didn't know what to do. I called my spiritual teacher, because I didn't even want to present. She said, "No, David, you traveled all the way there, come to share, and come to serve." And so I did. I got up on stage, and I was the tenth guy up there selling something. I'm presenting and going over how to present from the stage, and everybody was tuned out, not paying attention.

I had to use one of the Sell More tools. I was doing my presentation, and I was going to the credibility section. When you're presenting from the stage, when the authority speaks, people listen.

You want to be the authority figure. If I was speaking on stage, talking about real estate, and Donald Trump was speaking on stage, talking about real estate, who would people listen to more? Donald Trump, obviously. What kind of person is he? Confident and powerful. You want to make sure you're the authority and then 'be' that person.

As soon as I did that, they were engaged. But now let me tell what I really do. When I talk about Donald Trump or a celebrity or an authority, I point to myself, and thereby I associate myself with that authority figure and create a connection, establish my authority and credibility.

chapter 6

PART II: STORY

"A story is a trick for sneaking a message into the fortified citadel of the human mind."

—Jonathan Gottschall, literary scholar

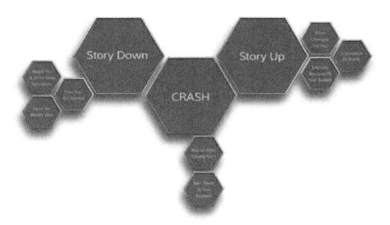

Story Down

- How You Got Started
- About You and Some Early Successes
- Facts Tell, Stories SELL

Have you ever watched a movie and been captivated, lost track of time, and felt like you were in the movie? Have you experienced that before? It happened to me. I was watching the movie Avatar, and before I knew it, I had lost track of three hours. I was in the movie. I was enthralled. A good storyteller can do the same thing from the stage. I can create a deep, meaningful connection so that people lose track of time. That is how a story should be told, when you connect to somebody in a deep and emotional way.

About a year ago, I met a gentleman at Dan Kennedy's Info Summit. There were about twenty speakers, including myself. This gentleman listened to all the speakers, and he saw about half the room run to the back when I finished. A year later, he said to me, "I can't remember anything about last year, but I remember you. You were the best speaker, and you know what? I remember your story." This is an entire year later, and there had been all those different speakers, but what he remembered was my story. Imagine that; telling a story that impacted somebody so much that they remembered me a year later. I made a deep, meaningful connection. That is the power of a well-told story.

Tips to Improve Your Storytelling

I'm sure you're wondering how to tell a story that captivates and inspires somebody so much that you make lasting impact and would be willing to write you a check. Stories are a covert way to sell. Think back to the story I told in Chapter Two.

My own story has plenty of ups and downs and pivot points. I overcame dyslexia and low self-confidence to earn a degree in sports medicine. I worked as a trainer for a professional football team, a job I loved — and lost when I broke my back, my wife left me and I was told I might never walk again. I learned to walk again! I started over with real estate and founded ForeclosuresDaily.com, which went nowhere until I was trained to speak. My company earned $50,000 after my first presentation! I built a team by training other speakers to spread the word about my business. At the peak of my success, I lost everything. I sunk my beloved boat, I was broke, hated, in debt; my house was in foreclosure, just one more listing on my own Website! So I started again with a new business partner, and here I am today, working with all the top speakers, debt free, creating value, being in service, giving back, deeply connected spiritually, loving my daughter and having fun.

1. Get Out Into the Audience

While telling their stories, most speakers make a critical mistake. They tell their story from the stage. The stage is the worst place for you to be when you are trying to get connected with your audience. When you're speaking on stage, an imaginary line gets created, resistance, you versus them. So when you tell your story, get off the stage. Come out into the crowd and start telling your story. "I grew up in Ann Arbor, Michigan, I had a great family, and in fact, my parents sent me to a Christian school…"

Now when I come off the stage and out into the audience, I make sure to connect with one audience member. When I connect with one, I connect with all. If you are a male, touch another male on the shoulder with the palm of your hand. If you are connecting with a female, touch the side of her upper arm with the back of your hand. Story time is connection time. The more people you touch, the more you connect at a deep emotional level. These are known as anchors. Open yourself up. This is vulnerability time. This is the time for you to go heart to heart. Speak from your heart, not your head. Come out and anchor and touch, because the more you touch, the more you sell.

2. Switch from Me-to-We

Start talking about yourself, and halfway through the story switch from "me" to "we." Using "we" highlights the essence of a shared experience. It's a two-way process that engages both the speaker and the audience. Remember, all buying decisions are based on emotion; they won't hear you, they'll feel you.

Switching from 'me' to 'you' during your story creates a transference. They will map your story onto their own lived experience. Now that you're telling the story, they will think it's about them.

Crash
- Pivotal Point/Turning Point
- What Changed For You

Ideally, the more failures you have had, the more vulnerable you are, and the better your story will be. Now here is the key. **When you tell your story, you want to have a crash.** Then when you take them down the crash, you want to have a pivotal point.

I've had many crashes, but the story I tell in my Foreclosures Daily presentation is about breaking my back, and thinking I was paralyzed. When I was in the hospital, I thought, "What am I going to do?" Then I anchor down my pivotal point. "Because of real estate, I did my first deal, and made $42,000. Imagine that. How many of you would love to do real estate and make $42,000?"

> "Story telling is story selling."

Here's the key. **If they trust you, they will buy from you.** The story is where you're going to develop the like and the trust. It should evoke the conclusion "I will buy his product." **You don't tell a story to tell a story. You tell a story to Sell More.**

Take Them to That Moment
What I'm about to write next is **the most important secret you'll ever learn**: When you get to your crash, you want to stop time. Take them to that moment. *"I'll never forget that moment waking up in the hospital."* *"I'll never forget when my boss let me go, or my spouse left me."* The most effective way to do this is by explaining the five senses. *How did you feel? What did you see? What did you hear? What did you touch?* You'll captivate us right into your story, we'll lose track of time, and then you'll take us to the pivotal point, which is, because of your product or service, X was possible. *"Since I began speaking for profit, I have made $14 million."*

Ideally you want to establish the crash, the pivotal point, and then you anchor down the product. You can point to it, or pick it up. I see people hold their product in their hands, or clutch it up to their chest. You may be thinking it's ridiculous, but it's gold. Remember what I wrote earlier, the human brain is like installing software in a computer.

Story Up

What Changed For You

"Story Up" is also known as the 'Hero's Journey'. This is a pattern of narrative identified by Joseph Campbell. It describes the typical adventure of The Hero -- in this case, that's you -- who goes out and achieves great deeds on behalf of the group or tribe. Remember your audience is your tribe. Describe what changed for you, the road back, your resurrection and speak about your results, the mastery of your experience, and link the results to the product or service you'll be telling in your story.

Lifestyle Because of Your System

Paint the picture of your story and how your product helped you overcome your pain and move up to the good life.

Importance of Family

The other thing that's important here is to have an audience that trusts you and build connections with them. Do you put family pictures in your presentation? It's amazing how the trust goes up when you do that. Trust builds rapport, all based on an emotional connection.

chapter 7
PART III: OFFER

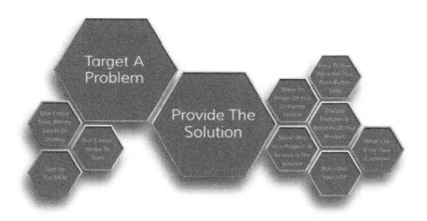

The Offer

When you present your product or service, do you wait until the close to tell your audience about it? The majority of speakers wait until the end to share their opportunity. That's not the appropriate time. That's like the pink elephant in the room. If you do that, they're not going to buy anything. Whether it's a webinar, a sales call, or on stage, the audience is sitting there thinking, "I know he's going to try to sell me something."

Right away I would get out there:

> *"Hey, my name in Dave VanHoose, I'm here to share with you some amazing tools and strategies about foreclosures." Within the first 10 minutes I'd say something like: "By a show of hands, let's play real quick with me, how many of you'd like to make more money, do more real estate deals, say yes. Let me see you guys."*

[The audience would respond with a show of hands.]

> *"By a show of hands, how many of you today want me to share with you and teach you how to get more profits and find more foreclosures, put them up and say oh yeah.*

[The audience would respond with a show of hands.]

> *"By a show of hands, how many of you here today think I might try to sell you something, put 'em up. Oh, that's it! Actually, I'm not here to try to sell you something, I'm going to sell you something. I am. I am going to sell you on taking your life to the next level. I'm here to sell you on buying and selling foreclosures. I'm here to sell you on having the life you've always wanted."*

They would laugh, and then resistance was gone. If you're talking to clients, the more transparent you are, the more the resistance disappears. "Hey, by the way, I have an amazing opportunity at the end of this presentation." **Ask their permission.** "Would it be okay with you if I share this opportunity? Would you be okay with that?" When you get their permission, the resistance is gone. The more you disarm them and leave space for them to choose, the more open they will be. But more on that later.

What happens is now they know what you're offering. Now during the whole presentation they're going "Well, I can see why that works." Now they can justify it through the whole talk. When they get to the end it's going to be an easier transition.

What most other people do, not you, is tell their story, teach about their product, try to sell the features about their product, try to sell their product. Teach, teach, teach, and then they'll get to the end and say, *Oh, by the way, I've got this very special book.* Nobody ever goes to the back to buy it because you didn't overcome the pink elephant in the room.

Do you think at the end of this book that I might have something to offer you? Well, I won't let you down, I do.

Target a Problem
- Don't Know Where to Start
- Don't Have Time, Money, Leads, or Strategy
- Turn Up the Pain

Every human being on this planet has one motive. What do you think that motive is? To remove pain. Everybody moves away from pain toward pleasure.

All you need to do here is target their problem and then offer them the solution. That's it. There is no selling. What most teachers do is target a problem and offer the solution as their subject. No, the solution is your product. Do you see the difference? The solution is you, your service, your coaching, your product, your boot camp. Stop selling and start solving problems.

What most salespeople do is try to sell the benefits. They'll move away from pain and then toward the benefit of your product. I have a saying: "Until you make them cry, they're not going to buy.

Provide The Solution
- Display a Graphic of Your Product/Service
- Show why your product is the solution
- Talk about the features and benefits of your product

- Easy-to-use, done-for-you, push-button is what sells
- What's in it for the customer?
- Point Out Your Unique Selling Proposition

What's different about you or your product from others that may be similar? Chances are, you're not doing anything new; however you're doing it better than 96% of the folks out there. The audience will naturally start comparing you with others so it's crucial for you to differentiate yourself. You need to answer the questions for them. What makes you different from Tony Robbins or McDonald's? You know what makes me different from Tony Robbins? Simple. Tony's focus is on self-development; mine is on sales development.

Note: Some of your differences may not be unique from every single one of your competitors, but this is OK, because in the end your product/service is different because you are different. So what makes your product or service unique? What have you included to go above and beyond your competition?

Bigger Reason

You have got to have a greater reason for doing what you do. Anyone can create a product or service, but why do you really do what you do? Think about what drives you to do what you do. Perhaps you want to save the world by recycling, maybe you have a charity, and maybe you've found something you're so passionate about you have to share it and watch as it spreads across the globe.

Now take a moment and collect your thoughts. What is your bigger reason? Write a simple sentence or two that really demonstrate your WHY, your bigger reason for doing what you do. If you prefer bulleted lists, write a few points. My WHY statement is simple: I believe in contributing & making a difference in the lives of the people I meet.

This helps your audience accept you at a deeper level when they see that your intention is to serve and not to sell.

When we host our 3-day or 5-day Mastermind groups, our bigger reason is: We're not here to help you with your business and teach you how to become a leader. No, **we're looking to empower you to become an amazing leader in a joint venture with us and to do business with us.** We find that the clients whom we teach end up being the best joint venture partners, and we team up with them.

The Law of Reciprocity

We all know that it's in giving that you receive. I always give stuff away during my presentation. I have a four-volume course, which includes *Volume I: Speaking For Profits*, all the check-lists, procedures, the how-to manual of putting on your own events, and the step-by-step systems. Volume II is Dustin's information on mass marketing, *Mass Attraction*. This includes the product funnels, the marketing templates, everything done for you. Volume III is *CrowdControl*: all the neuro-linguistic programming techniques I use, the tri- al closes, and the anchors. Volume IV, *Be a Rock Star*, outlines how to position yourself as a celebrity and become that go-to person in your field.

Let me ask you this question: if you're at a seminar, *How to Get Rich in Real Estate*, and you're passionate about real estate and you're sitting there and you win a copy of *How to Buy a House* and the rest of the course is available to you, are you going to go home without the other three parts? No. In my old Foreclosures Daily presentation I also had four volumes. It included *How to Buy a House; How to Sell a House; Land and Trucks;* and *Forms and Contracts*. When I was doing my presentation I would talk about them and then give one away. Guess what, I'd often make three more sales.

A long time ago, somebody gave me the movie called *The Secret*. I'd never heard about this "secret." I watched the movie and it really changed my life. I couldn't believe it. *Our thoughts can become things??* Coming from where I grew up, this wasn't the way I had been raised to think. The movie empowered me. Here's what I did: every time I spoke, my mantra was *I'm here to change one person's life*. And I would always play full out. I bought 1,000 copies of *The Secret*, and during my talk I would gift one copy to an audience member. It was a little game I played, figuring out who would get it. People sometimes called me back and said, "I was the one you gave *The Secret* to, oh my God, that changed my life. I did my first real estate deal after I watched that movie."

What's funny is I would say something like this:

> *"How many of you in this room have actually seen The Se-*
> *cret, put 'em up. Raise 'em. Who in this room has heard about*
> *it, but hasn't seen it yet? {And they would raise their hands}.*
> *Well great, here's my gift to you. It changed my life and I hope it*
> *changes yours."*

Then I did my presentation. At the end, I started noticing that whichever audience member had received a copy of *The Secret* was always one of the people who would run to the back table to buy. Could you, in your presentation, give something away? Your book, somebody else's book? Could you do that? Does that make speaking more fun? Do we help more people? Absolutely. The more you give, the more you make.

chapter 8
PART IV: BODY

"I didn't invent the hamburger. I just took it more seriously than anyone else. "

—Ray Kroc, founder of McDonald's

Teach 'Em the Steps to Succeed

- Break Down Subject Into 3 to 5 Simple Steps
- Make It Easy to Follow Your Process
- Tell the Audience What to Do, Not How to Do It

When you write your presentations, break your teaching down into five steps, or five keys, or five principles. Chunk it down, and make it easy. And alternate teaching with success stories. Write out five simple steps that when followed, your audience will know how to experience success with your topic.

Example: Steps To Personal Development Success

1) Discover Your WHY
2) Eliminate Negative Patterns
3) Increase Energy
4) Maximize Productivity
5) Celebrate & Share

Note: You want to keep your steps easy and simple. Consider this the Cliff's Notes version of your complete system. You're teaching WHAT to do not exactly HOW to do it, because you're limited on time --especially when you're speaking on a 45-70 minute webinar. Always make your last step something rewarding like Celebrate, Cash The Check, or Have Fun.

Create one slide for each step and go into further detail with your steps. This is where you get to shine your brightest and share your best strategies while still keeping everything simple, so it makes sense to your entire audience.

List some key points that you can expand upon verbally that outline each step.

For example: STEP 1 - Discover Your WHY

1) Determine where you want to live
2) How much money do you want to make?
3) Get clear on your goals.

I don't recommend having more than five points. You can always say more than what's on the screen, but always be aware of how much time you have left.

Reinforce what you teach in Step 1 with a testimonial. It's best to have a video of the person who gave the testimonial. If video is not available, use a picture of the person in written testimonials.

"Right now, for about the first ten & a half months of this year we've done about $10 Million in product sales with this web presentation we came to rebuild today, we anticipate in the next 12 months with this presentation I'd say we'll double that to $20 Million."

-Next Step Financial Holdings

Social Proof and Case Studies/Testimonials

Do you realize there's a difference between teaching and selling? Are you are a good teacher? I've got to show you how to become a better communicator so you are able to empower people into action. It's just a slight shift.

Here's where a lot of us have problems, because we think we need to teach, teach, teach, teach, teach, teach, teach, teach, teach, teach, teach, and oh, by the way, buy my product or service. How is that working for you? Not very good, I bet. I hear it all the time: "I don't get it, I built so much value for these people."

Are you wondering why teaching doesn't work? It's because you're teaching too much. Move away from teaching and towards storytelling. Here is the formula for successful storytelling:

- Teach
- Tell a success story
- Teach
- Tell a success story

The best way to overcome objections is through social-proof stories. The greatest salesman in the world is the best social-proof storyteller. When you watch an infomercial, do they teach you, or do they tell you success stories?

Let me ask you this. What are you more likely to remember, a story, or some information? Which one is more emotional? Do people buy teaching, or do they buy results? They buy results. So put some success stories in your presentation. And Engineer those testimonials, know what the objections are going to be and overcome them, because you're creating your case and taking people down a path, so that at the end of your presentation there's only one conclusion: I better run, not walk, to the back table and buy. Show checks of income or other proof of results when possible. **Make a note: You want to have seven case studies or social-proof stories in your presentation.**

These seven testimonials serve as social proof that your system has helped someone and case studies illustrating how it has helped. That will plant seeds throughout your presentation about the opportunity you are offering.

Here's a poor way to do a testimonial:
"Hey, the event was great. They were awesome. I love those guys!"

Here's a better one:
"I signed up for their program and within the first year, I made over a million dollars."

"Hi there, I'm Kevin Harrington. You may have seen me on the Shark Tank show on the ABC network. It's funny because I've been in the infomercial business about 28 years and I know how to find products, produce shows, and take them to the masses on TV, but it wasn't until I met Dave Van Hoose and Dustin Matthews that I really found out about the power of speaking and how important it is to work with experts."

What works about this testimonial is that Kevin is highly credible and successful, so sharing that he learned from us after 28 years in his industry helps establish our credibility. What could make it stronger is if he shared a specific result.

ROI Testimonial

You want to have testimonials that demonstrate a clear return-on-investment (ROI) and will let people know what they will get for their money. Social-proof stories should have a result: I made X amount of dollars, I lost weight.

> *"We just sold 17 packages at $1,497. A bunch more people are filling out forms and we are sorting out finances. We were Day 1 slot in 3 in London."*
>
> - The Lyttle Sisters, Alicia & Lorette, My Goldon Rolodex

> *"Just filled my Bootcamp Virtual Training where I used to charge $397 but this time I charged $797 and enrolled 12 people by tweaking My PowerPoint presentation using the Sell More techniques I learned from Dave and Dustin."*
>
> - Nancy Geils, Home Solutions Group

Plant seeds throughout your presentation. Testimonials will sell you and your product better than you ever could. Do people buy teaching or do they buy results? People buy results, so make sure you have them.

I've known Bruce Mack since the days of my old Foreclosures Daily. I used to do boot camps, and Bruce would come and talk about credit repair and how he would help people. We wrote one presentation for him. He made millions of dollars. This year he's building a brand-new software for salespeople that combines all the different social media and has this whole complete sales system for people. He's launching this new technology, and he calls me up and says, "Hey, I'm speaking at this huge conference in Vegas and I don't have a presentation." I said, "Well, you're going to have to write one, which usually takes about 50 hours to do correctly, or I've got the complete team and we'll do it for you."

He realizes it only takes one stage to get his ROI. In other words, he'll make the money he invested into his Power Day back the very first time he speaks. That's all it takes, one webinar, one stage, to get your ROI. We wrote his webinar. He was supposed to speak on the first day of this event. I found out there were going to be as many as 25 selling speakers, so I told him not to go, but he went. The promoter didn't know what he was doing, and Bruce's slot to speak kept getting bumped back. He was supposed to speak on Friday, but the promoter decided to put someone else up first and move Bruce to the afternoon. The afternoon comes and goes and they can't fit him in. Then it's first thing Saturday, but on Saturday they're booked up. Then they promise Sunday, and then it's Monday. Do you want to speak on Monday and be the last guy? Never. But he did. Here's what he says:

"What can I say? I've used Dave and Dustin. At my first event I sold over 40 percent of the room. I was the number one seller at the event. I out closed the top closer in the speaking industry. If you want some tools that work, if you want the help that's go-

ing to make the difference, absolutely give these guys at a call."

Wouldn't you love to be the top presenter on every stage?

Video Testimonials

When you get to the end of your presentation, I highly recommend that you have four or five testimonials building up to the close. You may have noticed that I have not-so-subtly been doing that throughout this book as well. I suggest you create a testimonial reel to include in your presentation with some of your clients' success stories.

To see more examples of social proof testimonials, go to
DaveVanHoose360.com/testimonials/

Use a Live Testimonial Whenever Possible

In-person testimonials are the strongest and most effective strategy. Use them whenever you can. Let's say you're doing an event in and you have some successful students in that city who are very happy with the results you've helped them create. Could you invite them and say, *"Hey listen, I'm going to be in Las Vegas. I would love to take you to dinner. I'm speaking at this event, would you come by, watch me speak?"* If you gave people a lot of results, what will they say? Absolutely.

While you're speaking, all you have to do is say something like this: *"Just curious. In this room, how many of you have been through the Power Day experience? For how many of you has it impacted your business in an amazing way, put your hands up, just real quick, I want to see. For those of you that have had phenomenal breakthrough results, if you believe in it and you're willing to give me a testimonial in front of everybody, just go ahead and stand up for a moment. I just want to take a quick moment. So, again, these are all the people that have come through a Power Day that you can talk to about it. They believe this. Thank you guys very much."*

A few months ago, I recorded a testimonial for the Speaker's Dream Team, aka the Closers. After I worked with them, it was such a powerful experience that I wanted to follow back up and let you know the results of the very first engagement I did after my training with them.

Okay, let me tell you, I had been at conferences before, where I had seen people run to the back of the room, and followed the speaker and get into a circle around them, and basically be throwing their credit cards at them, and that's exactly what happened to me. I'm sorry; I'm kind of giddy about it. It was really such a profound experience; you know, people were so excited about what I was saying, I know my message got across in a really, really profound way. My closing ratio went up by leaps and bounds, like 25 percent, which is again amazing. Actually I think it might have been even more than that, because not only did I sell product, I actually ended up selling a variety of my highest-level VIP days, my private days.

So it was really profound. If you are thinking about working with them, and I know it's a pretty steep investment, let me just tell you, I've made it back in my first engagement, my very first speaking engagement. And more important than the money was, now I have this opportunity to serve all of these great new clients that I would have never had that opportunity to play with before. So you guys, I am eternally grateful to you.

—Kelly O'Neill, Kelly O'Neill International and Marketing 2 Millionaires

Overcome Objections Through Testimonials

When your audience is listening to your presentation, they are naturally going to have an objection. And if they have even one objection, they won't be listening to anything you say. I call an objection an excuse.

The objection will be related to some belief they are holding onto, so you must address the belief. You could say something like this: "There are two types of people in this world—successful people and unsuccessful people. Unsuccessful people ask the wrong questions. They ask, *What does this cost?* You know what a successful person does? They ask, **"What is this going to do for me, and what are the benefits?"** We have got to overcome their objections. Anticipate all the questions and know your answers before you start. We need to overcome the resistance so at the end of your presentation the conclusion is "I want and need that" and they run to the back.

You need to figure out what the audience's biggest objections are. How do you know what they are? By asking them! At the end of your presentation or your webinar, find out why people didn't buy. They will tell you what the objection was. The most common objections are:

- I don't have the time
- I don't have the money
- That won't work for me
- I don't need it
- I'm too experienced
- I'm just a beginner

Your testimonials need to speak directly to the objections you hear the most often. Take the time right now to write down your client's four biggest objections:

_____

_____

_____

_____

When I did my Foreclosures Daily presentation, a guy came running to the back table and said, "You know, Dave, I'd get your system, but I don't have the time to do this." So I found a testimonial that said, "Hey, Dave, I took your foreclosure system, I did my first deal part-time and made $32,000."

One another occasion, somebody said, "You know, Dave, I would get your system, but I don't have the money to do real estate." So I found a client testimonial that said, "Hey, Dave, I took your foreclosure system, I did my first deal no money down."

Find case studies or testimonials and put them into our presentation to overcome those objections.

If you're having trouble with your objections and want a Sell More strategist to help you, go to www.DaveVanHoose360.com and receive a $500 coaching session free of charge for being one of our readers.

Show 'Em the Lifestyle
- Future Pace
- Show 'Em the Dream Life
- Tell 'Em You Believe They Can Have It, Too

The art and success of selling exist in getting somebody to experience your product in the future. Let me give you an example.

I shared with you earlier about the yacht I sunk. Well I bought a yacht about five years ago. I'll never forget, the salesman called me up and said, "Hey, Dave, I've got this beautiful Sunseeker, why don't you come down and take a look." So I drive down to meet him and I am so excited. I open the door and go back behind the boatyard. He says, "Man, look at this beautiful boat, picture yourself on this 50-footer. Imagine taking this out next week. Imagine putting your hand on the engine or the throttle, hearing the engine roar as the water comes shooting out the back. Imagine taking this boat down to the Keys and the Bahamas. You're surrounded by your friends and your gorgeous wife, sun shining, wind in your hair, without a care in the world."

He sold me. We'll go into more detail on Future Pacing in the Advanced Strategies Section of this book, but for now all you need to know is that he got me experiencing that boat in the future.

Show 'Em the Benefits

People Buy Benefits, Not Products

When you go to get a sales job and they hire you in corporate America, what do they have you memorize? The product. They'll have you memorize its features. Let's say they're selling a software program. "Well, this software does this, it exports here, it is going to do this, we are going to put it in here, this is what it will do. Look at all these great features that this software has." Do you think people buy the product? They don't. Do people buy features? No. **Why do people buy? They buy benefits. In fact, they buy the benefits of the benefits.**

What Does Your Product Do for Your Prospect?

First, answer the question, *What are you selling?* List the benefits and features of your products. Keep them short and powerful.

> *Example: The Abundant Wealth Empowerment Solution*
> 1) Easy Modules
> 2) Rapid Results
> 3) Financial Freedom
> 4) More Time
> 5) Greater Relationships

What are the benefits and features of your program?

MY ANSWER:
1)
2)
3)
4)
5)

One of the participants at a recent seminar was going to be speaking at a college about relationships. She was selling an audio program on dating and how to have good healthy relationships. So she is selling to students by presenting a message. The end phenomenon is an audio home study system.

The best strategy for her would be to say something like the following at the end of the presentation:

> *"I want all of us to consider, at this moment, the benefits of having a better relationship, having more fun, having better experiences, having more confidence. Picture this. It's a year from now and you are at the beach at sunset, and you're found the love of your life. You never imagined that it was possible to find this level of compatibility, attraction, ease and peace. You didn't think that you could be completely yourself and completely supported inside of a relationship." Build out the story. Sell them the benefits of the benefits of what it looks like with that perfect relationship and try not to sell the product."*

Do people buy what they need or what they want? **People buy what they want.** People say they need to get health insurance, but they buy a Gucci purse. It's so funny, we always try to sell people what they need. I know you need speaker training. But you don't buy what you need, you buy what you want. You want more free time. You want more money. You want to have more fun. You want to have a better lifestyle. So I tell them that's what speaker training will give to them. I sell them the benefits.

Have fun with this. Excite your prospect's imagination! Get them jazzed up about the future of their dreams! Answer the question: **How Can Your Product Improve Client Lives?** And remember, the benefits must address the prospect's hot buttons.

chapter 9
PART V: CLOSE

The close is one of the most important things of your presentation. A national average closing ratio for today's market is roughly 10 to 15 percent, but I know many speakers who only close 2 to 4 percent or, worse, 0 percent. Until they hired me, that is. A good speaker can close a minimum of 20 percent of a room. Some close 30, 40, even 50 percent. A lot of that depends on the personal connection you create with your buyers.

Live speaking events are one of the best ways to build relationships. Once someone connects with you, once they see you in person and meet you, they feel closer to you. You have a relationship. Couple that with a well-scripted presentation and an intentional close, and you are going to crush it in that room.

Let's walk through this.

Segue Into the Close By Asking a Question

Again, during your presentation, when you get to the close you want to provide a series of success stories, and then you're going to segue into the close by asking a question. You want to get another YES from the audience. After sharing 3 testimonials back to back I almost always ask, "Will YOU be my next success story?" When they say yes, they say yes to buying. That's a good part of your presentation as a commitment trial close.

Commitment Trial Close

"Picture this; what would it feel like to travel the world, have more fun, do the things you want to do in life? Imagine impacting the world at such a level and being able to spend more time with your family. What I want to share with you here in a moment is our complete speaker system, and this is not for everybody. I'm going to walk through the entire system with you so that you can get this, and then for some of you in this room you're really going to want to get this."

The purpose of getting the audience to picture the benefit of the benefit is to excite the imagination again right before the close of the presentation where you break down each of the items in your "Irresistible Offer". This slide would typically show four images that show the results of following your system. The pictures could represent lifestyle, freedom, wealth, happiness, or other desirable outcome.

To get a copy of your own Trial close sheet/flash card, visit **DaveVanHoose360.com**

Show an Image of Your Complete System

The purpose of this slide is to anchor the results you just spoke about to your product or service.

Following is a script of the Sell More Pied Piper close. I closed 80 percent of the room and we did over $400,000 in sales with this. Remember, the close ratio depends a lot on the quality of the people in the room. I told you at the beginning of the book that this is an experiential process. Keep in mind some of the Sell More techniques we've discussed and see if you can spot them.

"Would it be okay with you if I shared our complete system?
I've got my Platform Prosperity program, which comes with our

complete Power Day experience, and, here's what you're going to receive today. You're to get our complete Platform Prosperity program, and the benefits of this system are, you're going to have a professional team sit down with you and work with you step by step. It's going to help you convert more clients, get you on more stages, help you live in your passions, your purpose, take all the guesswork out, and it's going to really impact your business in an amazing way..."

Platform Prosperity Program
Including The Complete Power Day Experience

- Trained Eyes On Your Offer To <u>Maximize Your Profitability</u>
- **Save Time** - *You're On The Fast Track*
- Increase Your Conversions - *Increase Your Bottom Line*
- Take The Guess Work Out
- 10-Year **Proven System**
- <u>Tested Across Multiple Platforms</u>
- Get On Bigger Stages (Webinars/JVs)
- **Increase Your Cash Flow** - Financial Freedom
- Serve *More Customers*
- Get Your Optimized Message Out To The Masses
- *Done-For-You* By The Speaking Empire Team

Build Massive Value

- Build a "Stack" of All Components
- Provide Tremendous Worth
- Break Down All Components in the Complete System

"I've got my special program, which is 'How to be a Rock Star'.

"This program is going to uncover exactly how to position
yourself, how to become the go-to person—Dustin's going to
teach you exactly how to be a rock star. This system is valued
at over $1,995. You're going to really want this one. Who would
like to have this one right here? In fact, how about this, for the
first person that comes up here I'm going to give you this course
for free. I've got another something really important. This is my
crowd control, and you're going to really want this one badly.*

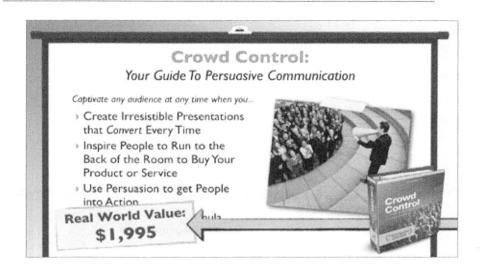

"This has all my neuro-linguistic programming techniques, the trial closes. This is going to show you exactly how to persuade anybody into action. Who wants this one? Again, this one is valued at over $1,995. Now, I've got something really cool. How about I go out so that I can make it fair for everybody. Why don't you sit down? I'll just give it to everybody so they don't have to run up. This one here is my mass attraction.

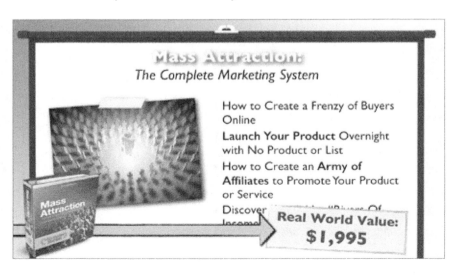

"This is Dustin's program. This will teach you about product launches; it will show you step by step all the marketing things. All you've got to do is plug it in. Who wants this? Let me see. You did it first. Come on up here.

"That one there is valued at over $1,995. I've got one more left. This is my favorite one, which is **Speaking for Profits**.

"This shares our organizational board, all our checklists, all our procedures, all our templates. This makes it so easy that a monkey could do this business. When we went public, we were required by our investors to create a checklist of systems and procedure for this whole business. So inside is our 300-game plan of how to put your next event on a check-by-check list so that anybody could do this. Let me ask you this question—who in this room wants this? Who in this room is going to do an event in the next three months? {An audience member raises her hand.} You're going to do an event? That's my gift to you. That will show you exactly how to do it.

"You guys want some more? In addition to that system, I've included something really special. We're going to give you the complete systems. Now how many in this room would love for me before I retire to personally write your presentation—just like I did the other guys'—so you have your script that will take you to the next level? How many of you'd be interested in that? Wow. That's too many of you. I can't do all that much work. Seriously, how many of you are going to be good students and have a product or service that truly is going to benefit the world who would like for me to write your presentations? Wow. That's a lot of you.

"So here's what we got in our program. I'm going to custom build your presentation. We're going to sit down, you, me, Dustin, and Leonard, my team; we're going to help you figure out your passion. We'll pull that out of you, help you create your system, build your presentation, all completely done for you. The really cool thing about that is you'll get to watch me present your product to you right in front of you so that you can see how it's done. And then before you leave you'll know exactly how you should be presenting. I'm your actor-speaker-coach—and you

walk out with your presentation done. From there, it's really easy. Just get on a stage or just do a joint venture and you're making money.

"How many of you like that product? Absolutely. That's a good one. It takes us a lot of time. It's not easy building these custom presentations but they're the most beautiful million-dollar presentations on the planet and we charge $15,000 for those. In addition to that I also wanted to include our game plan of how we did our sweeps across America. How many of you are thinking about going city to city to city to really launch your business in a huge way? This has how to make $103,000 in a weekend, our game plan, our scripts, the e-mail copy, the resource guide, everything we did. This one here's valued at over $2,500. This game plan is all you need to do your own seminars.

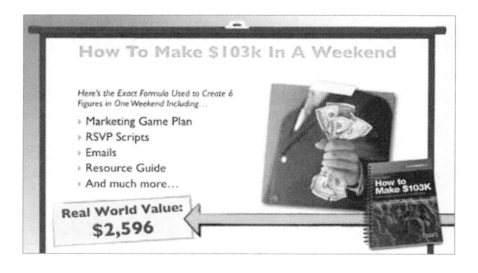

"I've got something even better than that. Who would like something even better than that? Well, here's what I want to give you: I want to empower you to be able to come to all our live trainings that we're doing across the world. We'll be doing events in Tampa, in California, in Russia, in Australia. We would love to have you be able to come to all these special trainings in this program, and here's what we'd love to empower you to do: get complete access to all our training in this special program valued at over $2,497.

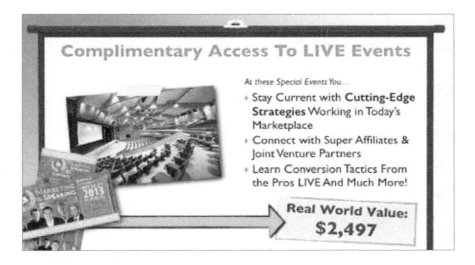

"I've also got something really special. How many of you'd be interested in learning my old script and seeing the most persuasive presentation on the planet? Well, the only way to get this one—people ask me for it all the time—is in this special offer today, I'm going to give you my $14-million script and I'm telling you you're going to learn all the persuasion techniques by reading my script and it will empower you. I consider that priceless. It took me seven years to figure that one out.

"So let's go over this.

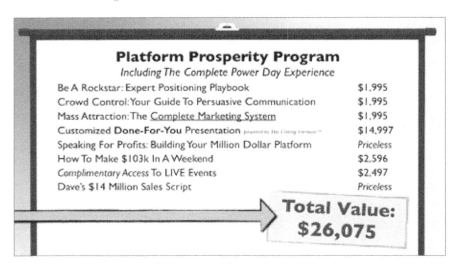

"You're going to get the Platform Prosperity Program. You're going to get Become a Rock Star. You're going to get Crowd Control, Persuasion, and Neuro-Linguistic Programming. You're going to get the massive track, the complete marketing. Basically *that means you have Dustin on your marketing team with all his marketing done-for-you. You're going to have the complete done-for-you presentation. We're going to build out your presentation so you don't have to do any of the work. Let us do all the heavy lifting for you. I'm going to give you this Speaking for Profits to share with you how to build your education business and share with you step by step by step how to do your boot camps, how to get the people to the boot camps. How many of you are excited about doing your own boot camps? You're going to really want that one because it's the complete game plan and we've also got access to all our live events and my $14-million script, which I think is priceless in this offer."*

Sell on Retail Value

What most people do when they get to their offer is discount it. **They don't get people to say yes to retail before they do a price drop.** This is a really key component, so let me run it by you. When you get to the offer slide, it's $10,000 today, but most people say it's not going to be $10,000, it's going to be $2,000. We've got to get them to say yes to $10,000 before we discount it. You have got to sell them on retail first. The most effective way to do that is by using If-All Statements.

Use at Least 3 "If-All" Statements

*"**If all the system did for you was** help you get on more stages and help you spread your message to the world and make more money, would it be worth the investment? Yes or yes? **If all the system did for you was** help you do your product launch or your joint venture and make you a million or even half a million dollars with the perfect presentation we created, would it be worth the investment: yes or yes? Absolutely. **If all the system did for you was** help you convert more clients so you could serve more people, so you could spend more time traveling the world, playing more, having more fun in your business, would it be worth the investment: yes or yes?"*

Special One-Time Discount

- Discount Good for Today Only
- What's the Reason for Discounting

You want to get them to say yes three times to retail. That way, when you do the price drop, you'll get the first wave of buyers. You want to close in waves because you'll close so well with the techniques in this book that if you get too many people to the back of the room at once, it can slow sales down. You have got to slow the process down because they can only process payments so quickly.

"So here's what we want to do; you look at an average college tuition, and you're going to spend over $85,000 to get a degree that will get you a job to make $25,000/year.

Average Cost Of A 4 Year College Degree...
$85,000

"What a joke that system is. Again, you can take the average franchise and buy a Subway and have a job.

Average Cost Of A Restaurant Franchise
$386,000

"Who in here wants that lifestyle? So today here's what we're willing to do: For the first five of you that get up, we're not going to charge you $26,000 for our complete program, and this is a year-long program of coming to all our events and the trainings and the complete system. This is a very special offer. It's not going to be $26,000 today. It's not even going to be $20,000 today. It's not even going to be $18,000. In fact, here's what we're going to do today: your small risk-free investment is only $11,997.

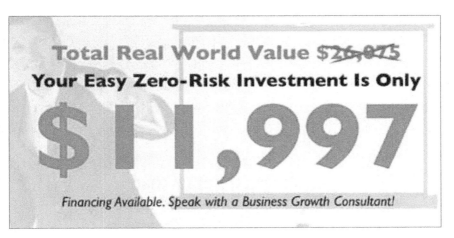

Total Real World Value $26,075
Your Easy Zero-Risk Investment Is Only

$11,997

Financing Available. Speak with a Business Growth Consultant!

"So you have my permission any time to get up and talk to the coaches in the back of the room, my friends, and this is an interview process. I've got to make sure it's a good fit for you and I've got to make sure it's a good fit for us."

Are You Worth The Investment?

"Now I want to ask you this question: Are you worth this investment? Is your family worth the investment? Absolutely. Then you know what you need to do, take action now.

Always Offer 100% Money-Back Guarantee
• Give a Personal Guarantee

"Now I believe in the system so much and I'm so passionate about your success that what we have is zero risk. What kind of risk? Zero risk. What I mean by that is when you sign up here at the program, we have you come all the way to our office. At the end of the day, if you're not completely satisfied with what we did, you just let us know and we will give you 100% money back guaranteed, no questions asked. Is that fair: yes or yes? Absolutely.

Promise To You

"You've got my personal money-back guarantee and my promise to you is this: when you check us out and you come do this, you're going to change your life. You're going to change our business. You're going to be able to get to that next level, I promise you that."

Fast-Action Bonuses

- Overcoming Financial Resistance
- Further Sweeten the Offer
- Special Bonuses for Those Seeking a Bargain

"Now, here's what I've got. There is a challenge we have. Obviously, we spoke at Traffic and Conversion and we're speaking here and we're speaking at several other events. My schedule is going to get booked up very fast.

"I have to personally write these presentations. So we can't do this for everybody. How many of you are considering this program? Put your hands up. Let me see. Just put them up nice and high. Wow. That's a lot of you. That's probably too many. So, here's what I want to do: I want to include some fast-action bonuses.

"How many of you would love for me to build your brand and let all the speakers in the world know about you to help you get on more stages? Who would like that? How many of you would love to send an e-mail blast out to our 50,000 speakers just like you around the world? Who would like that? Wouldn't that help you get on more stages? Wouldn't that help you with your product launch? So here's what I'm willing to do—I can't do this for everybody, but the first five of you to the back table—bonus number one, we're going to let you blast our list of all the speakers to get you on more stages. We're going to write the presentation. Step number two is to do what? Get on the stage. So we're going to blast our whole database for you about you. Would that help you?

"In addition to that, I also want to do something really special. I've got a radio program that goes out to all of our speakers and promoters in the world. Here's what I'm willing to do: again, for the first five of you, I'm going to put you on my radio show that goes out to all the speakers on my list. That's 50,000 speakers learning about you and seeing you as the expert. You can record that and now you've got your celebrity status. Does that sound pretty cool?

"How many of you like that one? Well, here's what I want to do: we've already got three people in the back of the room. Let's take the time right now. Let's congratulate all the smart success-ful millionaire speakers in the back of the room.

"Now can we do something even better than this?

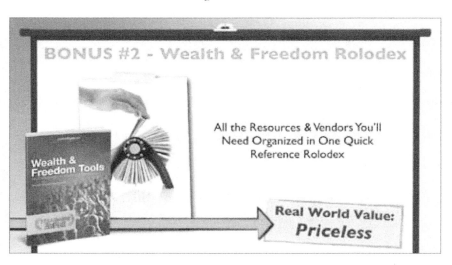

"How about this one: how about we open up our complete Rolodex to you; all the resources, all the people we use to help you and your business. This right here I consider priceless. How many of you will not have all the resources ready for you at your disposal? We're going to include that in this special offer, and this one you're going to really love.

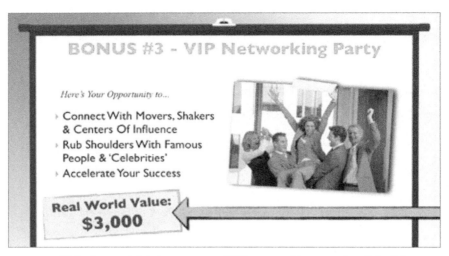

"We do special joint venture [JV] networking parties. We did one of them at Robert Allen's mansion in Rancho Santa Fe. People ask me all the time: Dave, can you get me on Robert Allen's stage? Can you get me on Russell Brunson's stage? The answer is yes. They're my clients and my good friends, but that's not a system for me. Here's what I know to be true: you become who you surround yourself with most, so here's what we do. We do special mover-and-shaker VIP parties. You're going to be able to come to all the JV networking parties included in this program to help you. How many of you like that one? That's a really good one, too.

"I've got another mega-mega-bonus. Who wants a mega-mega-bonus? How would you like to have my secret trial-close sheet?

"All my personal trial closes and neuro-linguistic programming techniques. You're going to really want this one. I've never included it before, and this is a $5,000 bonus. Who would like this one? I'm going to include it in this special program absolutely for free, but you've got to get back to that table.

"Now, how about this: before I retire, how many of you would love for me to personally do your presentation for you, in front of you, and record that?

"That way you can see somebody who's a professional speaker show you exactly how to sell your things. How many of you would like that one? Before I retire, if you get back now, I promise you I will be in your Power Day before I hand it off to one of my Sell More Certified Coaches to do. I can promise you that — which I consider priceless.

"So let's go over this amazing program again. You're going to get the complete Platform Prosperity program. I included four fast-action bonuses that you need to take action on now, today. Bonus number one: we talked about the instant buzz campaign. This one is put in there to help you get on more stages to help the world know about you and your product. That one alone, I'd be back there right now just to get that one. Bonus number two: our complete Wealth and Freedom Rolodex, all the resources we have. Bonus number three: the JV networking parties. Imagine being next to Robert Allen, Russ Whitney, all these top speakers and promoters. It would take you years to get in front of those guys. They're all there, so that way you guys can JV."

Second Call to Action

Tell Your Prospect What to Do to Invest

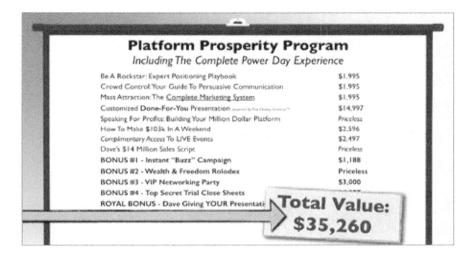

"I'm going to give you my trial closes and my roll bonus; I'll personally write your presentation and work with you to make sure you hit it, which I'll probably never do again after this event, and again, this is a $35,000 value. Today you've really only got three paths to take.

"One, you can sit there and do nothing and get what kind of results? No results. Two, you can try to write your presentation yourself, spend a minimum of 50 hours (what's your time worth?) and try to guess. Or three, you can just have it done for you. For me, I'm a done-for-you guy, and again it's not going to be $35,000. Your small risk-free investment is only $11,997.

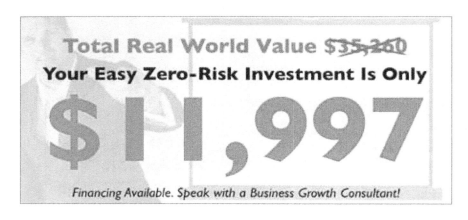

Give It All Away for Free *(Optional)*
• Refer X People and the System Is FREE
• Make a Deposit and Offer a Rebate
• Grant a Scholarship

"Now this isn't for everybody. We have some financing available so we've got something for everybody. Let me ask you a different question—how many of you would really love to get to the 4 percent club, grow your speaking business, put your hands up, say yes. How many of you would want this program and would want me to give you an opportunity to get this program and get it for free?

Would You Like To Get Everything For **FREE**?

"Anybody be interested in that? Put your hands up. Here's what I'm willing to do. Put your hands up. How many of you'd like to get this program, get signed up and get it for free? If you're serious, here's what I'm going to do: I'm going to go to the back of the room. I'm going to share with you how you can get signed up, and I'm going to share with you how to get this program absolutely free and be our JV partners. I'm going to go to the back of the room right now. You're already included because you're the first one. For those of you who want to get signed up and share, I'll show you how you get this system for free. Come meet me at the back table right now. This offer's going to end in five seconds. Five, four, three — come on. Let me show you how you can get this for free. Come on, come, come, come, come, come. Two, one."

Only You Can Choose To Join Me **NOW** At The Back Table.

{Speaking to the first audience member who went to the back table in response to being interested in getting the entire program for free.}

"My friend, so here's what we're going to do: I'm going to show you how you can get signed up, how we can help serve you and you can help us back. For the first five of you—I've got ten orders right here and here's what I'm willing to do: for everybody who's already signed up, you're already put into our partnership program. So if you're already signed up you're already in it. Here's what I'm willing to do: Dustin and I love to partner up with our clients. We love to do product launches and we love to do co-events with you, and we're looking for your help. So here's what we're going to do: how many of you saw what I did up there and would love to do that at your own seminar? Say yes. How many of you believe in our training and would promote this to your list or be able to help get us on another stage, put them up and say yes. How many of you would love to team up with us and maybe do an event or a webinar together, put them up and say yes. Here's what I'm going to do: I'm going to turn off my mike in two seconds so we can get all the serious people back here, but here I've got ten order forms. I'm going to share with you how we can get you signed up and give you an opportunity to get it for free. I'm going to turn off my mike in three seconds: three, two, one.

"We're going to share with you how to build your list, and we take the first $12,000 off the top so that you can get your system for free. Is that fair? Another way we're going to do this is doing an event. If you guys do an event, or we do an event and you come speak, if it's a right fit for us, we take the first $12,000 off the top and you get your system for free. We're looking for partners. We're looking for long-term relationships. I've only got ten order forms, and here's what we're going to do: we're going to *take a break for lunch. For the first ten of you we're going to take you over—this isn't a full commitment yet—and we're going to have lunch together. I'm going to explain to you how you can get signed up and become a partner and a JV with us and get this for free.*

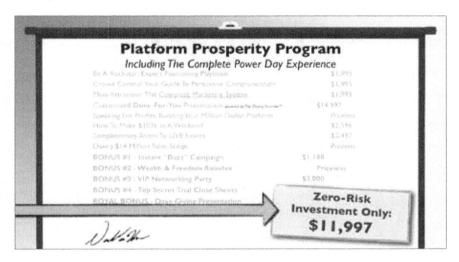

"So I've got ten orders. Who's in? {counts to ten}"

As you can see, the close is a build-up of energy that you unleash! This is how you create a frenzy of people running to the back table. If you were paying close attention, you would see how I inserted all the elements outlined in this blueprint. I grabbed their attention, I induced the yes state—I got them to say yes at least seven times, I made my offer irresistible, I built scarcity, I used my "if-all" statements, I sweetened the offer, and most importantly, I provided HUGE, undeniable value.

So my question to you is, *are you buying?*

SECTION 2
ADVANCED

Empowered by the Neuro-Emotional Empowering Patterns Technology

CONFIDENTIAL

Do not read past this point if you have not finished reading **Section I** *of this book.*

chapter 10
ADVANCED SELL MORE STRATEGIES

We're going to talk about very advanced language patterns. I'm really bearing it all in this book and showing you behind the scenes because I don't just want you to become a speaker; I want you to become a *conditioning expert*.

When I went to college and took a public speaking class, I didn't learn anything. I didn't even know how to conduct a job interview properly. It's important to be trained because all kinds of crazy things can happen when you're speaking, fire alarms go off, lights go out, people cough, cell phones ring, all kinds of things. You've got to have the training so that when it happens, you're prepared.

The majority of the communication in this section happens in the subconscious. In order to truly impact people, you want to communicate below the awareness, at a deep emotional level. I am going to break down these advanced techniques called neuro-emotional empowering patterns (NEEP) so they are simple and easy to use. I'm sharing the following strategies because you could get a crowd that's just not participating, they're a little tough, and you really want to make them move. You don't have to use them if you don't like. But you will have them at your disposal if you ever find yourself needing to engage your audience.

Mechanics of Body Language

When we present, we feel fear. Sometimes it grips us. The fear is there is because we are worried about our self-image. If we get rid of the self-image, detach from expectations, and make it about the audience and not about ourselves, the fear disappears.

What happens when you get nervous and feel fear is that your body's response is to tighten up and lock your legs out as a way of managing the stress, and then you're not breathing properly. This is a typical 'flight or fight' response. So when you feel fear, my best advice is to breathe. This is the secret to speaking. Think about a singer. A singer takes in large amounts of air, which allows her to project the voice. If you have oxygen in your lungs you will never stutter, you will be empowered, and you will be able to enunciate and speak with your own voice. You have a power voice.

Put the book down and practice this now. Stand up, shake your legs out, bend your legs a little bit, loosen up, and breathe in.

Do you notice any difference?

This may seem foolish , but trust me, this technique will serve you well in a room full of prospects.

Future Pacing

In my presentations, I always tell the audience that I want to share with them and teach them. This is called future pacing and setting the frame. Let's break down the mind and how communication works. There are two parts of the brain, the conscious and the subconscious. All buying decisions are based on emotion backed by logic.

How many of you have gone to the mall and bought one thing and then another thing and another thing, and you're driving home with all this stuff and you feel emotionally drained. But you back it up by logic. You say, "Everything was on sale! I needed this!"

Do you get that?

I like to take people down a path and if you can future pace them and take them where they can't catch you it builds the excitement. The audience is captivated and they're going to be hanging on to your every word, they're going to have way more fun and you're going to have way more impact. Future pacing would look something like this:

"Let me ask you this question. How many of you are liking this? Do you

Five Strategies to Engage Your Audience

Have you ever seen other speakers lose the audience halfway through their presentation? I have studied a lot of neuroscience, and the average attention span is about seven to ten minutes. That is to say, the brain will lose focus unless its attention is recaptured every seven minutes. Seven minutes! That's all you've got.

Any presenter that is failing on the stage simply isn't implementing a strategy every seven minutes to keep the audience engaged.

Strategy Number 1: Raise Your Hand. Get them to raise their hands every seven minutes.

Strategy Number 2: Write This Down. Have them write something down. You're going to say things like, "You're going to want to write this down. You can write this down now or later."

Strategy Number 3: Stand Up. Have an audience member stand up. "Stand up, turn to your neighbor, and say, 'You're amazing'. Turn to your other neighbor and say 'Let's have fun today'."

Strategy Number 4: Repeat After Me. Have them repeat what you've said.

Strategy Number 5: Turn to Your Neighbor. Have them tell their neighbor "You're awesome" or give them a high-five.

want more? Well I saved the best for last."

You want to repeat your offer so many times that it gets accepted in the subconscious state.

Do you have children? My little girl, Victoria says, "Daddy I want some ice cream." What do I say? No. Guess what she says again? Daddy, I want ice cream. I say no. She repeats it so many times, what do I do? *Yes, baby, here.* Children are masters at continuing to ask and plant the seed. We want to do this in our presentation. You don't let people know about our opportunity just once. You do it over and over and over again, and repeat it many times.

So during your presentation you can say, again, *"I have an amazing online funnel to automate your business. You know I have a great opportunity for you to take your business online. You know this amazing funnel will automate your time and energy."* Continuing over and over just like the ice cream.

A person says 'no' seven times before a 'yes'. So if you're a person that asks somebody once and then give up, understand that it's going to take six more times.

Anchoring

Do you remember when you were in high school and you listened to a song over and over again? I'm sure we all have a song that we grew up listening to. Take a minute now to think of a song like that. When you think about it, how does it make you feel? It takes you back. You might remember your mom, or your dad, or being in school. Your best friend. Your first love. Likely you have a rich and vivid memory or emotion associated with it. That song is an anchor. It makes you experience some emotion. You want to anchor your audience to an emotion during your presentation. **There are three places where you need to anchor: the product, the back table, and yourself as the expert.**

I used to love listening to personal development speakers on the plane when I did all these speaking events, especially Tony Robbins. There was a part where Tony says that most people die on Monday mornings. Did you know that? I couldn't believe that people can actually will themselves to die at a certain time. So I took this idea of the power of our thoughts into my presentation. As I'm trying to convince my prospects to get out of their J-O-B, in my mind I'm thinking that if I don't get them into real estate, they are going to die. That was my intention because I knew if they stayed in their job, it could mean death for them.

Tony Robbins said the number one reason for a heart attack is being in a job that you don't like, and I used to say it all the time in my presentations. After I was done, people would come up to me, hundreds of them, and say, *"Man, you remind me of Tony. You look like Tony."* *"What do you mean?! I don't have a big head and big teeth. What do you mean I look like Tony?!"* Now I look back and realize when I said his name, I anchored myself to him. So that's another tool in the toolbox. You can anchor yourself to create instant authority and credibility or instant celebrity status.

Stage Anchoring

I am going to talk about what side of the stage to put your product on and unravel the behind-the-scenes speaking secrets that nobody ever teaches.

When you are speaking from the stage, what side of you is the future? The future is to the audience's right, the speaker's left, because everybody reads left to right. What side of the stage do you put your product or service on? **The right side.** Are you getting that? Nobody knows these little tricks. When you have your product or service, you're going to put it in the future, on the right side of whichever way the audience faces. When you target a problem or turn up the pain, it is in the past. Have you actually ever considered that? When you tell your story or are turning up the pain, you want to be standing to the audience's left. That is stage anchoring.

Anchoring Down the Back Table

If you take nothing else from this book I want you to understand that selling is a simple, easy system. I told you how my company bottlenecked. I hired 25 other speakers to go on the road for me. While teaching them my presentation, there was a part that I knew worked, but I didn't know why. In my all Foreclosures Daily presentations, I used to say, "I have never ever, ever, ever, ever, ever, ever, ever, ever, ever seen a better time to get involved in foreclosures. The stars are aligned perfectly to do this business." The guys were like, "Dude, we're not doing this star thing, it's lame." I said you've got to do the star thing. I did not know why it worked. I just knew that it did.

When you can do something very well, that's one thing. When you are trying to teach somebody else to do it, somehow you have to give them the reason why. Now, I know why it works. While I was saying, "I have never ever, ever, ever, ever, ever, ever seen a better time to get involved in foreclosures. The stars are aligned perfectly to do this business", I would be anchoring down the back table. Where do you want your prospects to run at the end of your presentation? The back table. When you're speaking, if there's a point of sale, know that you have to anchor that down.

The Rolling Effect

When I first started speaking, I used to get so nervous. Before all my presentations, in the plane rides and the cabs, I'd always listen to some techno music or dance music to put me in a good mood and help me feel energized. I didn't realize it at the time, but the music would put me in a trance, just like the name says. I would then go on stage and do my presentation at the same pace as the music I listened to. And when I did the presentation in that pattern, people were captivated. In fact, they were hanging onto every word. The pacing of my speech would have them hooked through the whole presentation. At the end, I said, "Everybody get up right now and go to the back table," and they would not walk, they would run. Seriously. Remember, I had hired 25 speakers. I'm teaching them that they want to do my presentation in this pattern, like they're singing a song. They're wondering what I'm talking about. This is what's known as the rolling effect. Before you read this, you have to promise me you're never going to use this. This pattern's so strong I don't do it anymore because I think it's an unfair advantage.

Human beings breathe in and breathe out at a certain rate. When you talk at the same rate as they breathe, you actually put the audience in a trance.

Southern Baptist preachers speak in the rolling effect. Joel Osteen speaks in the rolling effect. President Obama speaks in the rolling effect. He's got the whole country in a trance, that's how powerful this is. I didn't know what it was; I just knew that it worked. The rolling effect is one of many ways to create rapport with your audience. It is a very important and quite an easy skill to master that enables you to get along with and influence any kind of person. Following their breathing patterns, mirroring his/her body language (not too obviously, of course) or using similar words as they use are all ways to become powerfully influential. Now, I am not suggesting you should do it and I do not want you to use it, but you should be aware of how powerful it is.

Scarcity

Scarcity is a very powerful persuasion technique. Limiting something causes human beings to take massive action. If you have two kids and there's one cookie left, we know the law of scarcity exists in a big way. When PlayStation comes out at Christmas, and they've only launched a certain number of consoles, people go crazy because they want it. **Scarcity works.**

Here is what I suggest. If you have scarcity, use it, but use it with integrity because a phony tactic doesn't work. Scarcity could be a great motivator. "Hey, for the first 20 of you that get up and go to the back table, I'm going to give you personal coaching session with me." Is your time unlimited or limited? Limited. You can only do so many sessions, right? That is scarcity and scarcity with ethics. We can use this, but just don't make up fake things.

When we do seminars, we only allow 100 people to attend and that's it. We don't like to have big events; we think smaller is better. We get to be intimate with you. We get to work with you, and our accelerated learning works better. The advantage to hosting smaller events is that the costs and the headaches go way down, and it's more fun. For your next event, when you book the room and they ask you how many people, limit it to no more than 100 participants. When you're doing your presentation, you could say you've only got 100 seats. Is that scarcity and with ethics? Absolutely.

Embedded Commands/ Direct Command Pattern

A lot of salespeople and speakers will try to sell two different things during the same talk. In other words, they give people two different decisions to make. This is a great injustice. This is one decision too many. **A confused mind doesn't buy.** This direct-command pattern will eliminate all confusion: tell them to go back and buy. **Tell them what to do and they will do it.**

Embedded Commands are a way to hide action commands in plain sentences and normal conversation that are processed directly by the unconscious mind. Everyone uses them to some degree, but most don't know they are doing it. Here are examples of embedded commands:

- Say yes
- Act now
- Learn this
- Order now

The list is a long one. Embedded commands are incomplete without phrases such as:

- You can
- As you
- When you
- You will find
- A person can

You can use the person's name prior to the embedded command for greater effectiveness. We are all conditioned unconsciously to respond to our name. "When you, Mr. Prospect, use our service you will find..." The word **you** and the **prospect's name** are the most influential words you can use in selling. Litter your presentation with embedded commands for a more compelling sales message and call to action.

Tone

Delivering an embedded command is as important as the command itself. It's crucial to incorporate the correct tonality in your voice to use embedded commands effectively. You can use the tone of your voice to bring about the outcome you desire. You want the tone of your voice to drop down at the end of the command. Speak in flat, commanding tones. I don't do rising tones at all because they're not as effective. Use pauses to drive home the point to your prospect.

Scotomas

Scotomas are what I call it when you communicate and connect at a deep level. Most speakers speak, and speak, and speak, and it's a one-way communication where they are speaking 'at' their audience. You want to connect in a two-way dialogue so the communication goes both ways. The more you can do that, the more you can stop and have the audience fill in the blank, the deeper the connection will be and the deeper the affinity you'll have with that person. When you are ready to give your presentation, don't be afraid to have the audience fill in the blanks.

Nonresistance/Covert Command/Persuasion Terminology

You want your audience to discover for themselves that they need and want your product. The definition of discover is to 'see, find, or gain knowledge of something previously unseen or unknown.' Discover means it was already there and you have simply been the channel for them to uncover it. When Columbus "discovered" America, it was there all along; only no one in Europe had seen it yet.

Have you have seen a show where a hypnotist put a willing participant into a hypnotic state and told him to bark like a dog, and the guy barked like a dog? That's the suggestion: the subconscious mind just reacts.

How can you deal with what I call conversational hypnosis? Conversational hypnosis is communication through the subconscious. We said all buying decisions are based on emotion. That is the subconscious. The conscious mind is the gatekeeper. So if you say, "Go to the back of the room," the gatekeeper can say "No." A statement like "Consider going to the back of the room" will bypass the conscious mind and go to into the subconscious.

These are what I call covert commands. Some examples:

"Statistics state,"

"A friend told me,"

"In my opinion."

"One could argue."

When you communicate using this persuasion terminology, you can communicate so that the audience hears what you're saying. It gets the resistance out of the way.

I want you to consider why the prospect might want this. And have them consider it: Here's what I would say to you, the reader of this book: "I want you to consider the benefits of doing a Sell More Power Day with me."

"You will notice yourself wanting to go to the back of the room..." They won't object when they are in nonresistance.

We do this in our Masterminds course because if you tell people what to do, they're going to break down, but if you give them a suggestion and they believe they originated the thought, they are more likely to do it. If you tell a kid to clean up his room, is he going to do it? But if he thinks he originated the thought, he will say, "Man, I should get my room cleaned," and do it.

Confusion Pattern

When I did my old Foreclosures Daily presentation, I had the thought that the more I put them in a confusion state, the more they responded to me. When I opened up something over here I said "picture this, imagine this," and I took them over here and I took them over there, and then I would give a suggestion like "real estate is the way."

When you put somebody in a confusion state, suggestions go into the mind automatically. This is a great therapeutic tool, by the way. Therapists can use this technique to empower somebody who's got a fear, about making money or swimming, allow them to get out of that self-limiting belief. A great way to do this is to say:

- Consider what you're not thinking right now.
- Remember to forget to remember.
- You don't have to believe me.
- You have the right to be wrong.

So you can have fun with it.

Presupposition

Presupposition is assuming something will happen before it does. When you tell someone what's going to happen to them, it will. By putting the idea in their head, you can make it happen.

"Get up and go to the back of the room."

Your audience will resist that statement. Every time. Humans are hardwired to resist a command. We don't like being told what to do. They will say no. So you want to communicate nonresistance. When you're on stage, what do you want your audience to presuppose will happen? That they will go to the back and sign up. Say instead, "Before you spontaneously run to the back of the room..." or *"Before you write a book with me, you need to know that I only work with clients who are really dedicated to completing their book."*

Make a note of this: you also want to use, **When you**. Sometimes listening to other speakers, I hear the words **"if you"** come back today, **if you** sign up. Not **if**, it's **when**. The word "when" presupposes, while the word "if" inserts doubt into the subconscious brain. This is also known as an Assumptive Close.

In the **assumptive close**, you act as if the other person has made the decision already. Turn the focus of the conversation towards the next level: Other examples:

> *"When will you be booking your Power Day?"*
> *"Which boot camp do you want to attend, the one in Tampa, or the one in Irvine?",*
> *"When you show up to the three-day boot camp, it's the most empowering boot camp."*
> *"When you look back five years from now, I want you to know you'll think it's the best investment you ever made."*

This technique is so effective that it doesn't really matter what you say after the presupposition. Remember, the gatekeeper (the conscious brain) is looking for any reason NOT to buy. So even one word will be the difference between your closing none of the room and your closing 40 percent of the room.

Power of Pause

One of the most powerful things that you can do is what I call the power of pause. When I was doing my Foreclosures Daily presentation, Dustin would literally bribe people to come see me. *Come down to the local steak house, Dave VanHoose is going to buy you a steak dinner and show you how to buy and sell real estate foreclosures.* Let me put it this way: the people who showed up weren't the best qualified. In fact, they were coming in cold off the street. I had a lot of work to do in 90 minutes.

I had to transform them from disgruntled persons listening to me speak into persons who would pull out their credit card and give me $8,000. In their minds, I knew that if I mentioned the word work, they weren't going to be a part of that. I had to get them to believe in themselves because they had a J-O-B. Convincing them they could turn their J-O-B into what I call their J-O-Y, which is starting your dream business, required me to shatter their disbelief.

During my presentation I used the power of pause. At the biggest climax or the most important point, you have to leave an uncomfortable pause that will have persuasive impact. I'd get them to say yes and then pause.

> At the biggest climax or the most important point, you have to leave an uncomfortable pause that will have persuasive impact.

At the climax of your presentation, if you can take them up that valley and get them to commit that they can do it and then pause, it'll be the most powerful thing you can do. A lot of speakers haven't mastered this and don't realize how potent it is. They puke all over everybody, and at the end of their presentation they almost faint. Remember, good speaking is an exchange back and forth. Make sure you pause. And during that pause, again, remember to breathe.

Emotional Timeline Experience

In order for the emotional timeline technique to be effective, you need to get into the world of your prospects. Take them back to the past on something they've already experienced—the first time they came to a seminar, the first sale they ever made, the first car they ever bought; you want them to remember what that was like. It can be positive or negative. When was the first time you lost a sale, when was the first time you spoke and nobody bought anything? This allows them to ground themselves in that emotion. From there, you want to take them on a journey with you, bring them back to the present, and then solve that problem or recreate that emotion in the future.

If you take nothing else from this book, remember this: *the art and success of selling exist in getting somebody to experience your product in the future.* Emotionally.

Time Distortion

By playing with time, you can put people in trances like hypnotherapists do. Time distortion might work something like this: *"Can you believe it's already been three hours that I've been talking this morning? Hasn't the time gone fast? Has the time gone fast for you? Absolutely, time's gone really fast."* Time distortion allows you to influence the audience by creating a hypnotic state. When they're in a hypnotic state, they can be influenced more easily and you can connect at a deeper level. Playing with time puts people in a hypnotic state.

Trial Closes

If you learn only this one strategy, it will raise you from a good speaker to a Sell More speaker. Very few speakers even know how to do this. Trial closes get your audience to say yes throughout your presentation. Have you been noticing my trial closes as you read?

> *Does this make sense?*
> *Are you getting this?*
> *How many of you are liking this?*
> *How many of you can see yourself being a successful speaker?*
> *Who wants to get to the four percent?*

In your presentation, ask "How many of you would spend $1,000 to make $10,000? In fact, how many of you would spend $12,000 to make $100,000? How many of you would spend $12,000 to make $3 million? How many of you would spend $12,000 to make eight figures, like Sam does?" You've got to have what I call an ROI commitment as the close.

I used to get my audience to say yes 68 times. Say yes, yes, yes. Condition, condition, condition. Is it making sense? Are you getting this? Trial closes are a nonresistant way to get the subconscious mind into a yes state.

***

And that is it! The best of the best of my ninja Advanced Sell More Strategies. **Mastering these strategies will get you on every stage ev-**

ery single time. Without a doubt, these are the missing link. If you master these skills, you will never have to worry about cash flow again, I can promise you that. I have trained a lot of speakers. In the last six years, I've written over 500 presentations. All these individuals are using my presentations, and giving me the results, so I know they work! I've got my finger on the pulse of exactly what is happening and what is changing on today's stages. If you're doing presentations, and having a hard time converting your speaking into sales, go to www.DaveH360.comand get one of our Sell More coaches to help you learn more about how to seamlessly incorporate these Advanced Patterns into your presentation.

If you're doing presentations, and having a hard time converting your speaking into sales, go to **www.DaveVanHoose360.com** and we'll get one of our Sell More coaches to help you learn more about how to seamlessly incorporate these Advanced Patterns into your presentation.

BONUS

Presentation Style Guide

Now that you've got all the tools you need to speak to sell and profit royally, you need to have the right visual presentation to go with it. When it comes to creating the absolutely best graphics and creative work, there is no one better in the biz than my creative director, Leonard Mello, so I've asked him to write a chapter on the finer points of building a compelling visual presentation.

The Importance of a Compelling Visual Presentation

It's been said that the first impression has to be your very best, because you only get one. What's the first thing you notice about anything or anyone? Is it the way something or someone looks? If you answered yes, then I urge you to consider what I'm about to share.

Dave has already informed you of the impact that dressing nicely and proper grooming habits can have on your performance, so please understand that your presentation is no less a part of your outfit than the shoes you choose or how you style your hair.

I'm a creative by profession; however, right now, think of me as your stylist.

Just Because They're Your Audience Doesn't Mean They're Engaged

Imagine for a moment that the most beautiful person you've ever seen walks into the room you're in. You stop whatever you're doing, and all of your attention is focused on one thing—the most beautiful person you've ever seen. Your first step to engage someone is to captivate her attention so she'll listen to your content.

This person also has the most soothing voice you've ever heard, and yet when she speaks, you're completely put off by the message. You're listening in disbelief as this beautiful-looking and heavenly-sounding person speaks—you're listening.

Engagement starts by getting your audience to listen.

Your message is irrelevant when nobody's listening. When you look the part, though, there's a much greater chance that even your most irrelevant message will still get listened to. So, the quickest and easiest way to captivate someone's attention is to stimulate her with powerful visuals.

In other words, you've got to make a strong first impression—you've got to dress your best and with a certain "style." Do you remember any first dates you've been on? I'm not sure about you, but I always, always look my best on the first date. If I went on a first date in my "comfy" clothes, I'm not sure how much of my "content" I'd get to share.

Great Content Doesn't Sell

It's an absolute privilege for me, and an honor, to work alongside such incredible Thought Leaders, who span so many different industries all across the globe, who all have amazing and interesting content. However, so many of the first impressions I get from the content I see are seldom impressions that would lead me down a path of wanting to know more.

Stated another way: *I'm not buying.*

It's never the content that sells; it's how the content is presented. This is where my passion to create visually compelling, interesting, and stimulating design comes in. I simultaneously apply many of Dave's subconscious sales principles with some simple effective design principles (which I'll share in a moment) to maximize engagement, keep your presentation interesting, and magnify the resonance your content has with your audience.

Now let's jump into this presentation style guide.

You've Got to Know How to Dress Yourself

You've got to know how to use your presentation software just as well as you know how to get dressed. There have literally been times when folks have come to us to craft their signature presentation for them, and when we ask if they use Power Point or Keynote, they have no idea. Other times folks have the software to create and play presentations, but the software is a much older version and unable to read the most up-to-date presentation file.

I implore you, if you consider yourself a speaker, stay on top of your tools. Update your presentation software when newer versions come out, and be sure you know at least the basics of how to use it. Not knowing how to use your software is like not knowing how to wear your clothes. There's nothing worse than being on stage and realizing that your shirt has been on backwards the entire time.

"You're Not Wearing That, Are You?"

Let's talk briefly about what you could consider putting on your slides. I often see people facing a lot of challenges when it comes time to dress up a presentation. Managing slide space is perhaps the biggest challenge I see.

Some folks put way too many words on a slide, which makes it really hard for your back-row audience members to see. This also reduces the retention of your message, because your audience wants to capture every last word on your slide—because you're the expert. If your audience is reading and writing, do you think they're also listening and writing? With too many words, you're forcing your audience to decide whether to take notes on what you're saying or copy what they see on the screen.

Too many words may also lead to people asking you to clarify or read the parts of your slide that they can't see or understand back to them. In some situations they'll even ask you to go back a slide (or sometimes two or more), because they were frantically trying to copy every last inkling of your knowledge. Ultimately this will only disrupt your flow.

As your stylist, I suggest you don't wear a lot of words on your slides. It's tacky. If you really want to wear all that, do it in a book. People will absolutely LOVE your words in a book. You can even wear some of that risqué stuff in your book.

What Colors Make You Stand Out?

I've found that the most important aspect of colors is consistency. You'll notice different templates you can choose In your presentation software; you can customize the colors or create your own templates as well. The purpose of a template is to give your presentation a consistent look and feel. I'm a strong brand advocate, so I suggest you use the colors that represent your brand.

For most of the creative work I do, I use shades of blue. Everything has a blue tint, from the pictures I use to the fonts I choose. The brand color itself is a very specific blue.

Now, there are a lot of different color theories out there, and every color means something different to somebody else, so I abstain from that conversation. I keep my focus on clean and simple design, and quite frankly I believe any color can look good on anything. If you're into statistics and you're testing colors, and you've found certain colors work better for certain audiences, then by all means use those colors. Otherwise, keep it simple, keep the colors consistent and in line with your brand, and it'll look great.

Wine Saved My Life

Isn't that an enticing headline? I saw it a couple years ago on the front page of a newspaper. Having enjoyed a glass of wine or two myself, I had to read the article, which is the ENTIRE purpose of a headline.

Nothing more.

Nothing less.

A headline is meant to stop someone in her tracks, grab her attention, and make her take an action. The action you want her to take when it comes to your presentation is simply to listen.

If you're going to put words on your slides, then what you want is a headline. You want a compelling headline with a thought-provoking image that leaves your audience no choice but to want to lean in and listen.

If there are any words on your slide other than a headline, people aren't fully listening to you because they're reading. You want to think like a newspaper without delivering a newspaper article on your slide. Newspapers use very vague headlines just to make you want to open up to that page. All of your headlines should give the audience the same feeling that pushes them to the edge of their seat, makes them want to listen and want to know what you're about to tell them.

5 Strategies You Can Use Right Now When Crafting Presentation Slides

1. Always Use Alignment and Grids

Keep things aligned on every slide. Grids are everything in design, because they keep everything clean, in its own container, and visually more appealing.

To help illustrate the power of grids and clean design when I speak to an audience, I always ask this question: Would you rather be in a clean room or a messy room?

Folks always prefer to be in a clean room. Knowing this, pretend that showing someone your presentation is like showing someone the rooms in your home that you're trying to sell.

When you go to sell a home, it's common that you paint, buy new appliances, fix anything that's broken, deep clean everything, put everything in its perfect position (according to the rules of feng shui), and make it look like the most pristine home anyone has ever seen.

It's easy to use grids to align things on your slides—in fact, your presentation software probably offers gridline and alignment solutions.

Here's a sample slide. The gridlines in red helped me align my bold headline SEXY, my words of wisdom "Remember Alignment (even in your presentations)," and the picture of myself to anchor the  word sexy to my likeness. (Thanks for the tips, Dave.)

Because I was discussing white space in design as a general topic, the background image is actually a two-page spread from a catalog. I could have just used the picture of the catalog; however, I wanted my message of alignment to resonate with my audience. To accomplish this and have my audience experience the grids first hand, I animated certain elements at certain times while I was speaking.

Which leads me to my next strategy.

2. Keep Use of Animations and Transitions to a Minimum

Ensure that your animations make sense and serve a specific purpose. Leave nothing to chance—don't use an animation just because it's available as an option. Used ineffectively, animations can be annoying to your audience.

Here's why I recommend you don't use animations. So many presentations I've seen have animated elements that come in at the wrong time, and it throws the presenter off. This most commonly happens because somebody moved a bullet without changing the animation settings, or maybe they moved a slide without changing the transition settings. Yes, animations and transitions are two separate things.

If you absolutely must use animations to make bullets or images appear, I recommend choosing a single style and using it for all the animations. The one animation I use all the time for both stage presentations and webinars is the APPEAR animation: you click and the element appears. It's not fancy, but it gives you control and the ability to "reveal" certain elements at specific times.

To recap, if you're using animation and you move any animated element, check your animation settings to make sure it still works the way you intend it to before you present your message.

3. Use High-Resolution Images

I'll keep this strategy super simple for you. Pay for the rights to all of your visual media no matter where you use it. Don't do a Google search and choose your favorite image; don't use a picture if you don't know its origin or who holds the copyright. You could end up paying anywhere from $1000 to $10,000 per picture. If you don't believe me, Google search: "image copyright fines."

4. White Space Can Stay White

White space is a blank area of the image. Used properly, you can lead the eye to look at specific places in your presentation. It creates a more dynamic visual appeal. White space is sexy.

In this catalog spread, I wanted to create a feeling of "this is all you need." There is no distraction on these two pages. On the left are the core components of a home study system, and on the right is the name of the system and a brief description. Just like a headline, this spread is meant to create a sense of desire, desire for the product or desire to learn more.

5. Keep It Simple

Keep it fun. Keep it honest.

Top Visual Mistakes

Now that you have some great strategies to make a visually compelling presentation, I want to leave you with the top two mistakes that you want to avoid at all costs when crafting a presentation.

1. Using too many fonts or fonts that aren't universal.

Don't just download a cool font and use it in your presentation (unless you save the font and bring it with you), because the computer you end up presenting on may not have that font, and it will change the formatting of your entire presentation. Has this ever happened to you?

I almost always use the Arial font family because every computer has it. It's very common, and it has enough versatility and variations (italic, boldface, boldface italic, etc.) for most presentations. Using a single font family keeps things consistent and clean. When you use too many different fonts, the slides start to look like they're not part of a single presentation. Subconsciously this creates confusion, and a confused mind doesn't buy.

2. Using low-quality images.

Do you enjoy the benefits of high-definition resolution? Would you trade in a flat-screen LED TV for an old tube TV from the 1970s? It hurts my eyes and my heart when I see cutting-edge content, information, and products that have an unintentionally low-quality feel to them. This happens when you use low-quality images or cheesy clip art.

Also, remember the fines for copyright infringement. If you're going to get fined for using an image that you found with Google, you should at least consider choosing a high-resolution image.

***

Success loves sequence, and now you've been introduced to the blueprint that so many others are using to make upwards of six, seven, and eight figures—sometimes in as little as 90 minutes. You have the sequence for creating your conversion mechanism (your presentation) and some simple effective design principles to dress it up in style. If it sounds like a lot of work, that's because it is. At least now you know where you can go to get it crafted in a single day.

Dave is always talking about the benefit of the benefit. The benefit of the benefit of a properly designed presentation is that you'll be remembered. A properly designed, visually engaging presentation is unforgettable. You'll impact more lives, you'll spread your message farther, and ultimately you'll make more money, so that you can truly experience the freedom you deserve.

conclusion

NOT CLOSING, BUT STARTING

In this book I have told you exactly what you need to do to Sell More. It begins when you connect with your audience, when you make it about them and what you and your product or service can do for them. As a speaker you need to take control, get your listeners engaged and involved. Get them to trust you, get them physically and emotionally involved in your presentation. Don't sell your product, sell the benefits of your product, and you will get them to act, to run to the sales table at the back of the room and buy what you have to offer.

Speaking is a learned skill set, and I have done years of research on how to do it effectively and have a high close ratio. From creating a framework to speaking at the right tone and pace, from anticipating obstacles and knocking them down to creating urgency, from putting your prospects in the future to positioning yourself as the authority who can take them there, my system will help you be a more effective speaker and successful salesperson.

I wasn't born a great speaker; I had to find my way through a maze of unsuccessful strategies and paralyzing fears. Now it's your turn. Let go of your fears and knock down the obstacles that keep you from achieving your dreams. Find a mentor, take a training program, figure out what you have to sell and how to add value to it so the package is irresistible. Learn the techniques of engaging, controlling, and exciting an audience when you speak. If you need help with developing a presentation or a strategy, help is available at DaveVanHoose360.com.

My life has been a roller coaster ride of ups and downs, successes and reversals. A broken back changed the course of my life completely when I was 30. I had to give up my work as a sports trainer, learn to walk again, and find something else to do. I found real estate. Many years and many failures later, I developed the Sell More system and techniques that are detailed in this book and am responsible for more than $100,000,000 in sales worldwide.

Now What?

I hope by this point in your reading you have a new perspective. I hope you see a way out of your J-O-B, out of financial stress, and that you're well on the path to freedom. I hope that you understand that speaking is about much more than selling, and that your product or service provides much more value to your client than a simple end result. You have a gift, and sharing that gift with others is a contribution to the world that creates value for those of us that can't do what comes so easily to you.

I hope you feel empowered, and are fully embodying your gifts, and speaking the unique truth to the audience like only you can.

Your success in life, your ability to be on stage and your ability to sell successfully from the stage is directly linked to your ability to be of the utmost service in this world. Your commitment to generating value is a commitment to success and freedom. When you provide value for others, you receive that back multiplied. Giving your audience permission to take action and change their lives and break free from the constraints that their fear has imposed upon them is a service to this planet.

I hope I have empowered you to take instant control of every audience, to spread your message and impact people on a deep, meaningful level. I have given you all the mechanics of the presentation—the blueprint, the script; the next phase is the practice. As with any skill or sport, all it takes to improve is practice, practice, practice.

When you learn start to learn something new—tennis, sports, speaking—you accumulate experience and training. As time goes by, you have more experience of being in tournaments or playing football games, or speaking on stages and with the right training, the coach will help you become the best in the world.

Experiential training is the most effective way to learn. You can talk all you want about strategy, how to win the championship game, but you've got to play the game to learn how to play the game. Now it's your turn to be successful by using the techniques I have developed. Let go of your fear and find the life you've always wanted. Learn to speak effectively. Book your first or your next speaking gig right away -- especially if you don't feel ready. The time is now to get out there and SELL MORE!

I'd love to meet you personally and have you attend one of our LIVE speaking events, or if you'd like me to write your Sell More presentation, visit www.DaveVanHoose360.com.

ACKNOWLEDGMENTS

I want to thank Dustin Mathews for being the best business partner on the planet and for weathering the ups and downs throughout our many years in business together. I can always count on him for his hard work and dedication. His talent and effectiveness in the marketing space have meant that I can go out and do my thing as a speaker. If it were not for him, there never would have been anyone in the room for me to speak to.

To Debbie Montis, for trusting me to start our first business together, for always being there, and for consistently being the glue behind the scenes that holds it all together.

Leonard Mello, thank you for all the graphic genius and creativity you bring to us.

Thanks to my ghostwriter Karen Rowe for helping me say what I had to say and making this book happen.

I want to acknowledge all the people who have been to my events over the years. To those who showed up, played full out, took action, and then went out there and made it happen. Your success stories are the reason I do what I do.

I would like to acknowledge my spiritual teacher Guruji Sri Sri Poonamji. You have helped me connect to my truth, step into my power as a leader, and embrace service and humanitarian work.

And to my daughter, Victoria, you are my world. Thank you for bringing meaning and sunshine to my life.

ABOUT THE AUTHOR

Dave is a true example of a winning spirit. Many attribute his success to his ability to accept nothing less than the best, and to his commitment to a mindset of abundance. It is this same focus on excellence that allowed him to play a critical team role during the 2003 Tampa Bay Storm Arena Bowl (XVII) World Championship season! His insistence on strong mental and physical commitment has provided him with the ability to overcome the many obstacles he has faced in his life, including complete paralysis at the young age of 29. His abilities to inspire leadership and provide speakers with the tools and strategies they need, continually raises the caliber of speakers throughout the industry.

Dave Van Hoose, is a master sales trainer and motivator. Dave is mentor and coach to some of the most experienced experts in the world.

His leadership and sales abilities took his first seminar based sales company, Foreclosures Daily, to number 35 on INC Magazines list of 500 Fastest Growing Companies. Within 3 years, Dave's company had 100 employees, over $30 million in revenue, and was producing 50-100 seminar events per month!

Dave has focused his business life on motivating world-class people to achieve more than they ever thought possible. His own achievements have led him to channel his success and energy into his new charity foundation.

Dave holds a Bachelor's of Science degree from the Eastern Michigan University in Sports Medicine. His accolades include winning theSpeaker Trainer of the Year award in 2010, and America's Trainer in 2011, and Platform Closer of the Year.

NOTES

NOTES

NOTES

The number one reason that people go out of business is because they don't sell. Speaking is the most Profitable Skill in the World. Yet more than 90% of speakers don't know how to connect with their audience. No connection = no sale. In Sell More: The Power of One to Many, Dave VanHoose shows you a step-by-step blueprint that will help you masterfully amplify your platform speaking abilities and put more money in your pocket.

In this book, Dave will show you how to:

- Sell anything to anybody
- Move and empower your audience to take action
- Use advanced persuasion techniques to get prospects to say "yes!"
- Create deep, meaningful connections
- Learn subconscious communication

At the end of this book, you will have a step-by-step system to engineer your presentation using a proven, scientific formula that guarantees results.

"It wasn't until I met Dave VanHoose that I really found out how important it is to deal with experts. Dave knows his business and he knows speaking. He's taught me a few things that I thought I had already learned a few years ago."
-Kevin Harrington
Chairman of As Seen On TV & original *Shark Tank* investor

"For 18 years I've been speaking on stages. Now my game is at a whole new level."
-Carla Ferrer
Coach Carla

About the Author:

Dave Van Hoose is a mentor and speaker coach to some of the most experienced speakers in the seminar industry. He has mastered the art of platform persuasion and personally delivered more than 3000 stage presentations.

His abilities to inspire leadership and provide speakers with the tools and strategies they need, continually raises the caliber of speakers throughout the industry.

www.DaveVanHoose360.com